Learning Social Care Law

by

Ashok Chand, Colin Fishwick

and

Helen Gorman

ISBN   0 948680 65 2

PEPAR
Publications

Contents Guide

The Authors

Ashok Chand is a Lecturer at the University of Nottingham teaching on a Post-Qualifying Child Care Award (PQCCA) course. His main areas of interest include child care law, anti-oppressive practice, social exclusion and social work assessments.

Colin Fishwick is an Emeritus Professor of the University of Central England and a former Associate Dean of the Faculty of Health and Community Care.

Dr Helen Gorman is a Senior Lecturer and Teaching Fellow in the School of Health and Policy Studies at the University of Central England, a magistrate and a former Approved Social Worker.

Acknowledgements

The authors wish to thank Chris Daines, Stephen Fishwick, Jerry Tew and Richard Steer for kindly reading drafts and offering helpful comments.

They also wish to record their appreciation to Lynn Spencer for her work in wordprocessing their various contributions to produce a coherent text.

Introduction

There are many books available which set out what social work and social care law currently comprises. There are some publications which advise lecturers how to teach social care law. There is less guidance around for those who are setting out to study this area of law or are making their early engagement with it.

We are three lecturers who have had extensive experience of supporting students with their legal studies on social care and social work courses. Our students have ranged from the very experienced to the complete novice, and from those who have previously studied the law to those for whom it is totally new. This experience has taught us that many students can enter into their legal studies and be expected to 'learn the law' without some basic concepts to help them. Similarly, we have observed many practitioners – without the benefit of formal training – who are expected to 'apply the law' but have no context beyond their own organisations in which to set what they know. As a consequence we have seen people struggling with legal aspects of their education and practice, and have had to help them use a basic idea to clarify the complex situations they are dealing with. We have written this concise book in an attempt to put some of those basic ideas together as a way of throwing light on the complicated legal issues which can be encountered in social care and social work.

So, we have set out to pose and answer a series of questions. As you will see, it is not our view that you should be told "this is the law, learn it, and you will be OK". Social carers, we believe, have to engage with the law in a more dynamic way. Although the book contains some social work law, it is not a social work law textbook. We have used the term 'social care' in a generic way to cover aspects of social work and health care as well as what we commonly mean by social care. This is because the ground we are aiming to cover is relevant to both social and health care professionals. For the same reason, you will find that we sometimes refer to social carers, sometimes to social workers, sometimes to health care workers, according to which is most appropriate in the context. It is also our way of trying to suggest that we want to remove some of the boxes in which we can so easily place the most important people of all – the service users.

The book's aim is to set you on the right track for learning social care law. We have attempted to do this by using as simple language as possible, and by making the ideas and information relevant to the experience of ordinary social care practice. We hope that it will give you a foundation on which to build your future studies and the development of your understanding of the legal aspects of your practice. Above all we want you to be enthusiastic and curious about the legal framework of your practice, not frightened or intimidated by it. Go on ... engage with it! Many others have stood where you now stand, and we have stood alongside them. We hope our book helps you feel you are not alone in 'learning social care law.'

Chapter One

Why 'Learning the Law'?

This chapter explains why it is important that those who work in health and social care should have an understanding of the law. It then goes on to explain ways in which the law relates to work practice. Learning the law is much more than memorising facts and repeating them; one could say that an understanding of the law is at the core of professional work in health and social care in terms of –

- the need to act in the service users' best interests;

- the representation of the users' voice (advocacy);

- the significance of ethics and the principles of fairness;

- a recognition of a variety of rights and responsibilities;

- the importance of following the correct procedures in matters that relate to the public;

- evidence-based practice: the importance of giving sound reasons for action.

Having a knowledge of the law is important; equally important is developing skills that relate to the application of the law in practice. By learning the law and applying it in practice situations, opportunities should arise for challenge and debate. The legal system is there to deal with conflictual situations when they arise. Often, in health and social care settings, differences emerge between various parties which result in recourse to legal rules and precedents. The world of health and social services in the UK is one that has increasingly recognised the role of the 'market.' Welfare pluralism – the provision of services by the public, private and voluntary sectors – is now commonplace. Clients and patients are more aware of their rights as consumers, they may be more prepared to challenge decisions made by professionals and formally complain about services that they have received or not received. Sometimes such complaints turn into legal disputes. The advent of the Human Rights Act 1998 links our laws to the European Convention on Human Rights. This means that it is more important than ever that those working with vulnerable people have a good understanding of the law for their practice in health and social care.

● Is learning the law about understanding rights and obligations?

It is certainly true that learning the law means understanding people's rights within the framework set down by Statute (Acts of Parliament) and increasingly being aware of the interpretation of the Statute by the Courts (case law). However, it would be naïve to assume that the interpretation of rights is self-evident. The rights of one person usually impact on the rights and duties of another and this can cause differences to emerge. The law has to be interpreted and this can involve a complex web of dynamics that depend upon the perspectives of those involved. In Chapter Five we will look at the duties and powers of local authorities. In certain circumstances local authorities are duty bound to do certain things, at other times they can use their discretion: for example, whether or not to provide services to older people in the community.

It is possible to argue that all rights and duties are not necessarily legal rights. Any interpretation of rights and duties leads to a consideration of ethics. For example, in health and social care there have been a number of highly publicised cases where hospitals have refused to give certain treatments, as when a child dying of cancer was refused expensive drugs (Child B). Should the child have been given the treatment using resources that could have been used to save someone else's life? How do you decide who should be treated and who should not? Should smokers be last in line for lung cancer treatment? These are moral dilemmas that relate to rights and responsibilities of individuals and organisations. Professional practice is dependent on the interpretation of the law and it is with the use of discretion in interpreting the law that ethics – the rules controlling the conduct of people in relation to others – come into play.

Nevertheless there are certain rules that have been established in law to ensure that society functions in an organised way. For example, if you go to court as a professional worker you may have to give evidence as a witness. There are certain procedural rules that apply in courts of law, for without them there would be chaos and the likelihood of unfairness. There are basic rules of fairness, for example "the right to a fair trial", which exists in the law of Evidence and Procedure but has now been reinforced by the Human Rights Act 1998. Other rights within the European Convention – such as Article 8, "the right to family life" – if contentious, will be viewed in the context of domestic law; so for example, a residence order for a child will be decided under the terms of the Children Act 1989 and its associated practice guidance.

Many people go into the caring professions because they have a desire to help others. Part of the work is making sure that when you intervene in people's lives you give them accurate information and advice. It is important that you help them to be aware of their rights and advise them about the systems of welfare, which can be complex and difficult to understand. It is therefore your responsibility to be aware of rights and obligations and to have an understanding of their meaning in context.

● *Is learning the law about "getting it right first time"?*

This phrase has become synonymous with the notion of 'quality'. When we intervene as professionals in the lives of others, it is possible that we get involved because society says we should, not because that person has requested our help. An example of this is when a social worker acting as an Approved Social Worker has to detain a person who is mentally ill against their will because they are a danger to themselves or others. In a situation like this, a social worker is charged with great responsibility; s/he needs to know exactly what the law says and what her or his powers are. S/he also needs to be aware of the rights of a person who is ill and the rights of the relatives of this person. One cannot afford to make mistakes or be vague about powers, because to do so may put a person's life at risk. The same point can be made about child protection: decisions have to be made that have a sound legal basis for action. So, in that sense, professional workers need to know and understand the law and how they should apply it. They also need to know the law as it relates to the roles of others; for example there are legal rules that apply to the psychiatrists and nurses who treat someone detained under the Mental Health Act 1983.

- Learning the law is about precision. It does matter that certain words or phrases are used in law; they are there for a purpose. It is true that certain terms used in the law, for example 'needs' and 'significant harm,' do have to be interpreted, but there are precedents (case law decisions) that help to clarify meanings. That is not to say that there will never be a difference of opinion as to the interpretation of meaning in context.

- When learning the law, it is important to understand legal references such as the sections of an Act of Parliament: for example:

  section 47 National Health Service and Community Care Act 1990
  (*This section of this Act is about assessment for community care services*).

- It is so important to get the date of an Act right, especially when Acts of Parliament have similar names. It is also very important to distinguish policy papers from the law. One classic mistake is where students refer to the "law" when they mean a policy document such as the White Paper entitled 'Caring for People' (1989). This was an important document because it set out the policy framework for the changes that were to take place in the way that services in the community were organised. However, it is not 'the law'. The law is in the National Health Service and Community Care Act 1990 (NHSCC Act 1990), which followed some eighteen months later. Sometimes policy is not translated into law; a good example of this is at point 2.9 of the White Paper 'Caring for People'. Here a reference is made to the importance of taking into account the needs of black and ethnic minority people; however the NHSCC Act 1990 does not make any reference at all to this, unlike the Children Act 1989 which incorporated this point within the statute and therefore made it "law".

● An Act is usually divided into Parts and then into Sections. This allows for easy reference and for clarity about meaning – when we refer to s47 of the NHSCC Act 1990 we know we are talking about the assessment for community care services. It is also important that you recognise that sections can be divided into subsections, written for example, s47(1).

● When referring to cases, it is important that you use the case reference. Over the past ten years or so, the application of the law in health and social care has become more contentious. One can speculate on the reasons for this. It is possibly to do with a raising of awareness of people's rights which can only be a good thing; on the other hand a lot of the disputes have come about because of a lack of resources available from Hospital Trusts and Social Services Departments. Usually cases that come to law emerge through a process of Judicial Review (see Chapter Five). Cases are often expressed as, for example, R v Avon CC ex parte M 1993. This means that the case was brought by the Crown, written in a case as R (Regina – the Queen or the State), against (v) Avon County Council. The case was about M. The use of the initial is because that person was deemed to be vulnerable and the name was not exposed to the public, and the proceedings took place in the child's absence. These references have common currency and are understood by all people involved professionally in the law – they are shorthand ways of being clear about the origins of legal principles.

● Is the law about recognising the conflicting demands of practice?

There is an increasing volume of law that relates to work in health and social care. It is necessary for some practitioners to have a very specialised knowledge of law, for example in respect of the adoption of children. However, whatever your role and work context within the health and social care arena, it is likely that you will come up against tensions and dilemmas in practice that relate to differences between values and legislative intentions. Often we look at the law to provide some clarity in situations that are muddled and sometimes a successful resolution of a problem is attained. At other times the complexity and variety of interpretation of the law causes more confusion. A very good example of this is the problem associated with meeting the needs of those assessed for community care services because of claims by local authorities that they do not have sufficient funds to supply services. What should determine the quality of service provisions – people's needs or the availability of resources?

The very nature of work in health and social care relates to people who for various reasons are in need. They may be in need of protection, they may be in need of care, or society may consider (expressed through a local authority and the agent of the local authority, the social worker) that an individual is in need of control. Various laws may apply to a situation where control is thought to be needed that may be in conflict with the caring aspect of a social worker's role. Similarly, an older person's right to remain in his or her home even if it is insanitary and dangerous may conflict with the risk that such persons present both to themselves and their neighbours. It is true to say that the law upholds the 'status quo'; it is probably true to say that the law reflects certain prejudices within the society. There have been changes in the law that shape attitudes and behaviour, for example the Race Relations Act 1976, Sex Discrimination Act 1975, Disability Discrimination Act 1995. Some would argue, however, that these laws do not go far enough. It is also possible for Acts to be made which are not fully implemented, for example sections 1-3 of the Disabled Persons (Services, Consultation and Representation) Act 1986. These sections would have given greater rights for advocacy to disabled people.

So sometimes the law may help to clarify 'the rules' but at others interpreting the law can be difficult because the law is live – it is constantly being changed to reflect society's view of a particular problem. It is therefore very important that practitioners keep abreast of the changing laws that are relevant for good professional practice. It is wrong to assume that the law is 'certain'. It does give rules on which to base practice but it cannot give all the answers – the world is more complex than that. It has to be a matter of interpretation. What is important is that those involved in working professionally in health and social care appreciate the complexity of the law in context and are confident to make decisions that affect other people's lives in a way that can be supported by evidence.

● Is the law about good professional practice?

Professional workers in health and social care are not mini-lawyers. They operate within legal frameworks and their job roles are related to their functions bestowed on them through their employment – for example, as social workers or nurses. However, it is one thing to know the law, it is another to apply it to practice. In becoming a competent professional worker it is essential that such a process takes place and that novice workers are supported by supervision in the agencies. This means that experienced workers also need to be updated; it cannot be assumed that qualified workers will always be fully aware of legislative changes. It is each practitioner's responsibility to make sure that as professionals they are aware of the current laws that apply to practice – the dangers of not being aware are too great.

Good professional practice means learning from experience – our own and others. Being on your toes in a situation that demands an interpretation of the law in practice means being able to work professionally whilst understanding when you are out of your depth. Sometimes situations will be so complex legally that it is essential that lawyers are involved, and part of being professional is understanding when such a situation arises. This can happen now in almost every branch of practice in health and social care.

● Why do we need to share our legal knowledge?

We need to be confident in the part we have to play in working with others in the health and social care arena. More so today than ever before, we cannot work with clients in isolation; indeed the government has repeatedly emphasised the importance of inter-agency work through policy documents and the law. The Health Act 1999 specifically enables joint funding and joint commissioning between health and social services to promote a 'seamless service' offered to users and carers. One professional cannot be the only source of information and support to an individual with complex needs and it is vital that in risky situations each professional is aware of her or his role and responsibilities in relation to decisions taken. Very often the social worker has a statutory role to play and needs to ensure that both the client and her or his fellow professionals are aware of their statutory powers and duties. At the same time, the social worker needs to be aware of the legal powers and ethical responsibilities of other personnel such as doctors and nurses who have significant powers and duties in relation to shared clients. An example of this is the power of the Responsible Medical Officer (RMO) in the discharge of patients from hospital following a compulsory admission under s17 of the Mental Health Act 1983 as amended by Mental Health (Patients in the Community) Act 1995 Sch.1 paragraph 15.

● *How do we apply the law and make legal principles work?*

The term legal principle relates to a rule that holds true when applied to a set of similar but different circumstances. It relates to the notion of legal precedent which means a judicial decision that serves as an authority for deciding a later case. It can also mean that certain legal principles are incorporated in statute law – for example the notion of the avoidance of 'significant harm' in child care encapsulated in the Children Act 1989. However, as has been discussed previously, legal principles, although extracted from a sound evidential base, are open to interpretation and re-interpretation in a developmental spiral; the law is not static and remains open to re-interpretation in a judicial context.

The student coming to learn the law for the first time can be faced with the dilemma of firstly understanding a legal principle and then applying it to the real world of practice. It is possible to lose touch with the reality of the law – that legal principles were derived from real-life situations in the first place. Much can depend on how learners make sense of their learning. Some of us engage with learning on the basis of our previous experiences; what we experience and what we learn are closely bound up with one another. Others of us tend to engage with learning based on concepts and theories that we have learned from reading and previous learning. Kolb (1984) recognised that people can enter the learning cycle at different points, but at whatever point they enter, the cycle remains the same; it relates to experience leading to reflection then to conceptualisation then to application and back to experience and so on.

When you engage in learning about law and social work law in particular, the skills you develop are essential for any professional practitioner. In order to apply the law to a given context you have to think laterally; you have to apply 'rules' to a different but similar situation. It is something that professional workers do on a daily basis – the secret is knowing whether a rule applies (based on knowledge of the law) and then making a decision about whether it is relevant in the particular case in point. This process requires a number of skills which are part and parcel of learning about law. It is vital that those learning the law develop skills in clarity of expression. In law the interpretation of a word or a term is of critical importance – precision in the use of language is important. By learning about law and applying it in practice, the opportunity arises for the development of this important skill. Being able to express oneself clearly relates to an ability to think clearly and give a rationale for the views that you hold; this is another way of saying that statements need to be evidenced – that they need to be based on more than a whim. In addition it is important to be aware of the thought processes that underpin your rationale. The ability to think logically, to follow one thought or idea to another through a process of reasoning, is essential if a student is going to engage in the process of learning social care law and make sense of it in the practice situation.

Chapter Two

What Do We Mean by Law?

● *Why have laws?*

The usual answer to this question is that two features of the human condition make law necessary. First, the world has relatively scarce resources and, second, our interests do not fully coincide. So, given the world as it is and us as we are, there will be conflicting demands; to avoid chaos or worse there must be ways of regulating these conflicting demands – hence we have rules or laws.

● *Who makes the rules or laws?*

It would be simple to answer this question by saying: "rulers make the rules". Then we are quickly into big debates about who the rulers are: a dictator, the 'boss class' or, in a democracy, the representatives of the people. Much of this chapter is about where our laws come from and what we mean by law in the United Kingdom, because the answer to the question 'who makes the rules or laws?' is much more complicated than the simple one given here.

● *Are there any universal laws?*

Would it not be a good idea to have one set of laws, applicable to everyone in every land? Well, philosophers and jurists (those versed in the science of law), have struggled with this question over the centuries. International law looks at the relationships between countries and the rules for governing those relationships. The Charter of the United Nations concentrates on state sovereignty rather than individual rights, hence how can international law intervene in sovereign states? How do we get universal agreement on human rights in a world where there are competing ideologies about what is best for humankind, which reflect different political, social and cultural priorities?

The Universal Declaration of Human Rights issued by the United Nations in 1948 has found particular expression in the European Convention for the Protection of Human Rights and Fundamental Freedoms (referred to as the European Convention), and this has now been incorporated into the law of the United Kingdom (from October 2000) by way of the Human Rights Act 1998. But what this Act does is not so much to introduce new laws but to establish an *approach* to how existing laws, procedures and practices are applied. When people talk about rights, there is often a struggle between two different approaches: one which emphasizes freedom from interference (especially by the state and its officials) and one which emphasizes what others (especially the state and its officials) should do by way of active assistance to enable human beings to flourish. There are, therefore, two competing views of individual liberty: the negative approach supports freedom *from* interference and argues that we maximise liberty by minimising interference; the positive approach argues for freedom *to* realise our potential by providing effective opportunities.

So, as can be seen, we find ourselves discussing *issues* rather than just stating universal rules with which everyone agrees. Such issues can easily be seen in the 'law' relating to social work. For example, should families be left alone to bring up their children as they wish, with some believing in 'spare the rod and spoil the child', and others in a 'no smacking' policy, or should the state intervene – through its officials such as social workers – to determine the rules for how best children should be enabled to flourish? Similarly, should we all be left alone to make our own arrangements for how we live our lives in times of sickness and old age, or do we have the right to state services (such as community care) to enable us to have as fulfilling lives as possible at such times? If we go for the positive approach, then who pays, and how much? Social care law is very much about finding answers to these sorts of issues and questions, rather than applying simple universal laws on which everyone agrees.

● *Where do the laws apply?*

Because there is no easy universal law to apply, different laws apply in different places. In the United Kingdom there are different legal systems for the different countries which make up the United Kingdom. There are different legal systems in Scotland, Northern Ireland, the Channel Islands and England and Wales. The laws included in this book relate to England and Wales, although with the recent devolution of some powers to the Welsh Assembly more differences may now develop in the legal systems of these two parts of the UK.

Each area where laws apply is known as a 'jurisdiction'. So, where Parliament, Secretaries of State, Local Authorities or others have powers to make rules, they can only make them within their jurisdiction. Local Authorities, for example, can make certain bye-laws which apply only to their area. But in an increasingly mobile and networked world, the interconnections between different jurisdictions are becoming more important. European law, as we have seen, now plays a very significant part in English law. For social workers there can be the complications of inter-country adoption, with very different notions of what adoption means in different jurisdictions.

● *What do we mean by law?*

Having seen that the main question being considered in this chapter is not a simple one to which a simple answer can be given, we can now look at it in more detail.

As we have seen, the law exists to regulate how we behave as citizens in a world of limited resources and of differing needs and aspirations. The *criminal law* governs our behaviour as citizens in respect of society in general, and the *civil law* governs our relationships with each other, as family members, as employers and employees, as landlords and tenants, as neighbours and so on. The courts which deal with criminal matters are usually the Youth Courts, Magistrates' Courts and the Crown Courts. Those for civil matters are usually the Family Proceedings Courts and the County Courts. But there are also higher Courts, some of which are Appeal Courts. A criminal matter can end with someone being found 'not guilty' or, alternatively, being found 'guilty' and then punished with one of a range of penalties. A civil matter usually ends with an 'order' requiring someone to do something or stop doing something, or to pay damages to another person who has been wronged.

But what is important to note at this point is that a 'legal person' need not only be an individual, but a legal person can be an entity such as a company, a local authority, a university, a Board of Governors, or an office-holder, such as the Home Secretary, a Director of Social Services or a police constable, or an Approved Social Worker. These entities or office-holders can be given special powers or duties under the law which allows or requires them to do certain things which others are not required or permitted to do. In fulfilling these functions they can, like the rest of us, fail to do what they should, or not do things properly, or abuse their position, or try to exceed their powers. Thus, like lots of other people in various positions, social workers and health care professionals can fail to fulfil the law, abuse the law or try and exceed the law if they do not know and understand the law as it applies to them. That is why learning social care law is so important to those who take on the role of social worker or social carer.

So, we ask the question again: "what do we mean by law?" We have already seen that it is hard to get universal agreement on how we should live together and treat each other, and thus what ideas and policies to enforce through the law. While most people agree that it is a good idea not to kill each other, and we make murder a most serious criminal offence, all killing is not illegal – even under the European Convention – and so we distinguish manslaughter, death by dangerous driving, accidental death, unlawful killing, and so on, and need other rules to govern warfare, riot, effecting a lawful arrest or preventing the escape of a person lawfully detained, and other situations.

In order to turn our ideas into law, the process in this country is usually to pass laws in Parliament, although it is increasingly important to remember the place of European law as a source of our law. What Parliament does is to make *statute law*. Normally, political parties issue their manifestos at election time saying what they propose to do if and when elected. If a particular party has a majority of Members of Parliament, it forms the Government and sets about putting its plans into action – much of it through law-making. Often the process begins with the publication of a *Green Paper*, which discusses the issues and proposals in ordinary language. This is a discussion document used for consultation with those interested in the particular subject. Following the consultations, the Government normally produces a *White Paper*, in which it sets out its plans in a fairly finalised form. Then when it is ready, a *Bill* is produced, putting the plan into legal language for consideration by Parliament. To become law, a Bill has to go through several stages in Parliament, where it is discussed in both principle and in detail, with amendments and corrections made in the process. The stages are:

>*First Reading* – the Bill is introduced by the Minister concerned or by a backbencher and its name is announced.

>*Laid on the Table of the House* – the Bill is printed and distributed to Members of Parliament and other interested people.

>*Second Reading* – the principles and main aspects of the Bill are debated fully in the House.

>*Committee Stage* – a Committee (of the whole House for money or controversial Bills or of a Standing Committee for other Bills) discusses the Bill in detail, clause by clause.

>*Report Stage* – if the Committee was a Standing Committee it reports back to the House.

>*Third Reading* – the finalised version of the Bill is finally debated and a vote on it is normally taken.

>*House of Lords* – if the Bill is passed in the House of Commons, it goes to the House of Lords, where it goes through a similar process of three readings and Committee stage, or vice versa if the Bill was introduced in the House of Lords (which occasionally happens with less controversial legislation).

>*Royal Assent* – if the Bill passes the House of Lords, it goes to the Sovereign for the Royal Assent.

>*An Act or a Statute* – with the Royal Assent given, the Bill (with its 'ideas' now in legal form) becomes an Act of Parliament, known as a Statute, and so becomes the law of the land when it is implemented.

We have to say 'when it is implemented' because the arrival of a law on the Statute Book does not mean that it applies from day one. For example, the Children and Young Persons Act 1969 had a controversial element in it – to raise the age of criminal responsibility – which was passed by the Labour Government just before it lost the General Election of 1970. The Conservatives, who had argued against this during its passage through Parliament, then chose not to implement that part of the Act when they became the Government, and so social workers at that time had a major piece of legislation in statute which did not apply, while the remainder of the Act governed important areas of their work.

It is usual for Acts to be implemented in stages, often because the resources or facilities are not in place immediately. A good example is the Crime and Disorder Act 1998, where several of the new 'orders' which could apply to young people were piloted in certain areas of the country to test them out before they were applied across the land. This is achieved by the Act giving the relevant Secretary of State the *power* to implement the legislation at times of his or her choosing. This is done by what are known as Commencement Orders. So, in such circumstances, what applies in Norfolk may not be the law in Northumbria for a while, or part of an Act may be implemented nationally, but there can be a time lag before other sections are implemented. It is not sufficient therefore simply to turn to a statute to find out what we mean by the law.

One Act can, of course, amend a previous Act. Again, it is not sufficient, therefore, to go to an Act of Parliament and say: "there it is, in the Act, it must be the law!" It is necessary to keep up with changes in the law. It may be found that, when implemented, the law does not work out as intended, or some refinement or development is necessary. Therefore opportunities are taken when related legislation is being passed through Parliament to make amendments to earlier legislation.

Acts of Parliament are not the only sources of the law. In the United Kingdom we also have what is known as the *Common Law*. It gets its name from the creation of one system of law in place of numerous local customs and practices in earlier centuries. It now refers to the substantive law and procedural rules which have been created by the judiciary through the cases they have heard over the years. So the Common Law is judge-made law, as distinct from statute law produced by Parliament. So we have in this country many legal principles which lawyers and courts apply to situations where legal judgements have to be made when there is no specific statute covering that situation.

Which brings us to the other main source of the law: *Case law.* This is the law that comes from judges' interpretations of statutes and the application of Common Law principles in specific cases. The cases are recorded in the Law Reports and used as precedents in similar cases in the future. Therefore, although there may not be a law to cover every situation, there are lawful ways of deciding what the law should be in any given situation. For example, the Children Act 1989 laid down in statute that when a court decides any questions in respect to a child "the child's welfare shall be the court's paramount consideration" (Children Act 1989 s1(1)), but an unanticipated situation arose in one case in Birmingham. The court had to decide between the interests of a 16-year-old girl who was in care and those of a baby which she had. Both were children; whose interests should be paramount? The House of Lords decided it had to put the welfare of the baby above those of the mother because it was dealing with an application concerning the baby not the mother. (Birmingham City Council v H (No.3) (1994) 2 WLR 31). This is the reference to the case, so that lawyers know where to find the Case Report on this matter, because it has in effect said what the law is in such circumstances. All reported cases have references for this reason.

A word of caution here. The traditions outlined here about how the law is made in the English legal system differ from the traditions in much of Europe. We have yet to see how the law will develop as the different traditions increasingly emerge, especially with the implementation of the Human Rights Act 1998 from October 2000 onwards.

● *What are Duties and Powers?*

Social workers have been called 'creatures of statute', meaning that the idea of a person or role called 'social worker' has been created by statute law, and so can only exist in terms of what statutes say they are empowered to do. Some professions have their name protected by law, so that it is an offence for someone to set themselves up as something which they are not qualified to be, such as a medical doctor. Some professions are regulated by statute, setting out the nature of their professional responsibilities and how these are to be governed. Social work, however, is not currently like this, but comprises a range of duties and powers which have been given by Parliament to various authorities and individuals. Following the passing of the Care Standards Act 2000, however, a new body, the General Social Care Council (GSCC) will be established from 1st October 2001. The GSCC will be responsible for promoting high standards of conduct and practice among social care workers and high standards in their training by registering the social care workforce, publishing codes of practice for social care staff and their employers, and approving courses in social work.

It is important to understand the distinction between a duty and a power. Where a statute imposes a duty on a person or a body, then it has to be carried out; where it gives a power to do something then the person or body *may* exercise that power but they are not obliged to do so. Many statutory duties and powers in social work are laid by statute on 'the local authority', not the individual social worker. The Local Authority Social Services Act 1970 made it a requirement that local authorities establish a social services committee, which was to deal with social services matters, and that they appoint an officer to be known as the director of social services. Consequently, many social work duties and powers are vested in these statutory bodies and persons. Individual social care workers carry out many of their functions on behalf of these statutory bodies through their contract of employment with them. In fulfilling some other duties, such as those carried out by Approved Social Workers under the Mental Health Act 1983, the duties and powers are vested in the individual social worker. The question 'What are Duties and Powers?' is answered more fully in Chapter Five.

● How different are the roles of central government and local government?

Every time a social care worker takes something from a day centre store cupboard or a field social worker makes a home visit – and when both get paid – somebody's money is funding the activity. Usually, it is public money. The right to spend public money is prescribed by law. Central government can only spend money on those activities which Parliament authorises it to do by law. So each Secretary of State must act within the law. Acts of Parliament lay duties and give powers to Ministers in the same way as they do to other bodies and persons like local authorities and directors of social services. Often the legislation says what our taxes can lawfully be spent on. Once again, the issue of what citizens should do for themselves and what the state should do for them arises.

Increasingly, what central government does is provide the money, set the legal framework and general policy in an area of activity and hold other bodies (like local authorities) to account for what they do within that framework. Local authorities then either deliver the services themselves or (if they can lawfully do so) pay others to deliver them. For example, they often fulfil their duty to deliver certain social services by arrangement with voluntary organisations or private firms. It is in these ways that local government fulfils the duties laid on it by Parliament.

When they have been given a *power* to do something, ministers and local authorities are allowed by law to spend our taxes on various activities, but they may choose the extent to which they do so. It is for this reason that some services vary considerably from area to area: they are lawful, but they are not absolutely required. Central government sometimes puts pressure on local government to do things which they are empowered to do but if the local authorities are slow to do so, it uses ministerial powers to force them, or in some instances, changes the law (through Parliament) to make what was a power into a duty. This happened, for example, when, following the Utting Report on Children in Public Care (1991), the Secretary of State for Health acted on a recommendation in the report and asked local authorities to produce and publish plans for children's services. This was done by issuing a Circular in November 1992 – LAC(92)18 – to this effect, advising local authorities to draw up plans. In 1993 the Social Services Inspectorate began a survey of a sample of such plans and published its analysis in 1995 (SSI 1995). Meanwhile the Audit Commission published its report, "Seen but not Heard" (Audit Commission 1994), recommending that the Government should take a lead in raising the status of children's services plans. In response, the Children Act 1989 (Amendment) (Children's Services Planning) Order 1996 was made under section 17(4) of the Act. What section 17(4) of the Children Act says is: "The Secretary of State may by order amend any provision of Part I of Schedule 2 or add any further duty or power to those for the time being mentioned there." It can be seen then, that by using a power given in the Children Act 1989, the law was developed – in the light of reports and enquiries – in a way which resulted in a new duty being laid on local authorities to assess the need for provision in their area of services under Part III of the Children Act, to consult with various bodies in planning how that need will be met and to publish the resulting plans. So, if you see a copy of such a plan in a social services office, or in a local library, our taxes have been lawfully spent on producing it, and what is more the local authority had a legal duty to produce it – it was not just some manager's bright idea!

We return in Chapter Four to consider in more depth the relationship between legislation, policies, circulars and guidance, after we have taken a closer look, in Chapter Three, at what we mean by an Act and some of the Acts which affect practice. From having read Chapter Two, we hope you now appreciate why there has to be a fairly long answer to the question "What Do We Mean by Law?" and have some understanding of why we have laws and where they come from.

Chapter Three

What Do We Mean by an Act?

● *What is an Act of Parliament?*

We saw in Chapter Two how an Act of Parliament comes about, and noted how Acts can be implemented and changed. We also noted that they are called Statutes, and that the courts interpret statutes as they go about the business of applying the laws of the land.

When an Act has been passed by Parliament, it is published by Her Majesty's Stationery Office and is on sale to the general public. Every Act has a title and a citation (now the calendar year). In practice, Acts are commonly cited by reference to their short title, conferred on them by a section in the Act itself.

It is not possible for a court to go behind that which Parliament has enacted, in order to make a statute illegal or to change it, but courts have to interpret at times what an Act actually means. The parliamentary draftsmen who write the Bills and Acts can sometimes be ambiguous, unclear or apparently contradictory, as they seek to put into legislative form and legal language the ideas which the Members of Parliament want enacted in law.

Sometimes, when an area of law has become complicated, a 'consolidating' Act is passed. Consolidation Acts are not subject to parliamentary debate, but special procedures are used to ensure that they do not depart from pre-existing statutory provisions. Such an Act, therefore, should not introduce any new law, but should tidy up the legislation to make it more understandable and easier to manage. When child care law became what one commentator called "a tangled thicket", it was drawn together in the Child Care Act 1980, much to the relief of practitioners at the time. But in due course it was completely repealed by the Children Act 1989 which introduced a whole new approach to the law in respect of children. A similar thing has happened recently with the coming into force on 25th August

2000 of the Powers of Criminal Courts (Sentencing) Act 2000, which draws together the law in respect of the sentencing powers of the criminal courts.

Since 2nd October 2000, however, when the Human Rights Act 1998 came into force, all UK legislation must be given a meaning that fits with the European Convention on Human Rights, if that is possible. If a court decides that it is not possible, it will be up to Parliament to decide what to do.

What Acts affect social care?

In Chapter Two we said that social workers have been called 'creatures of statute', meaning that they can only do what Acts have empowered them to do. That is why social workers in social services departments speak of their 'statutory' work. Of course social workers in other settings may do non-statutory work. There are many Acts of Parliament which lay down the duties and powers of social care and health care authorities and their employees. This book is not a social and health care textbook. It is an aid to learning social care law. What follows in this chapter is not, therefore, an exhaustive list of the Acts which affect social care. The aim is to give a snapshot of some of the relevant legislation in the four main specialisms of social work: child care, mental health, youth justice and adult community care. In this way, it is hoped to illustrate how the statutes and the principles which underpin them come to govern the work of practitioners.

What is the main Act governing Child Care?

When we talk about child care social work, it is difficult not to think about all the media attention over the years that has criticised social workers for removing children from home unnecessarily, or for returning abused children back home where unfortunately they have been abused again. What is important to recognize here is that the law, in this case the Children Act 1989, is actually very child-centred and states in a comprehensive way how children should be supported or protected in different situations. So why do social workers make so many mistakes? Well, in truth, they don't; what the media portrays are the worst cases that were mismanaged and led to the death of a child. Whilst this minority of cases should not be minimized, there needs to be a balanced approach of reporting the majority of good work carried out by social workers with children and their families. As already stated, the primary legislation that governs child care practice in England and Wales is the Children Act 1989. There are a number of principles that underpin the Act and these will be explored here in some detail, along with an overview of some of the areas covered by the Children Act 1989.

● *What are the principles of the Children Act 1989?*

● *The Welfare Principle*

This is stated at the beginning of the Children Act 1989 on the first page. It is the guiding legal principle for courts that deal with child care cases and states:

> s.1(1) 'When a court determines any question with respect to –
> (a) the upbringing of a child; ...
> the child's welfare shall be the court's paramount consideration.'

When considering the child's welfare the court should refer to the 'welfare checklist' (s.1(3)) which details seven points to help them decide what is in the best interests of the child in question. These points include the child's wishes and feelings (given his or her age and understanding) about what is happening; a child's physical, emotional and educational needs; the likely effect of a change of circumstances for a child e.g. being removed from home; and how capable a child's parents or carers are in meeting their child's needs.

● *No Delay Principle*

Often when cases go to court there is a great deal of time that passes from the start of a case through to its conclusion. In some circumstances, cases can take years before a conclusion is reached. With regard to children, this second principle aims to protect children from their court cases being unnecessarily delayed:

s.1(2) 'In any proceedings in which any question with respect to the upbringing of a child arises, the court shall have regard to the general principle that any delay in determining the question is likely to prejudice the welfare of the child.'

● No Order Principle

In addition to the principle of no delay, the no order principle states that:

s.1(5) 'Where a court is considering whether or not to make one or more orders under this Act with respect to a child, it shall not make the order or any of the orders unless it considers that doing so would be better for the child than making no order at all.'

● Parental Responsibility Principle

This principle recognises that a child's parents and not the state have overall responsibility for their child.

s.3(1) 'In this Act 'parental responsibility' means all the rights, duties, powers, responsibilities and authority which by law a parent of a child has in relation to the child and his property.'

This principle should not be under-estimated since social workers often cannot become involved with children without parental consent and agreement. The main exception is if social workers have evidence that a child is, or might be, at risk of suffering significant harm. They can then apply to court for an order that gives them parental responsibility (PR), though it is shared with the parents. The only time a parent can lose their PR is when their child is legally adopted. It is also important to note that birth mothers always have PR for their child, unless of course their child is adopted, but this is not true for natural fathers. This chapter does not go into detail about PR and how it is obtained, but further information can be obtained from most childcare law books.

● *What are some of the main duties under the Children Act 1989?*

● *Children in need*

Under s.17(1) of the Children Act 1989 every local authority has a duty –

  a) 'to safeguard and promote the welfare of children within their area who are in need;

  and,

  b) so far as is consistent with that duty, to promote the upbringing of such children by their families.'

The Act goes on to say (s.17(10)) that a child shall be taken to be in need if –

  a) 'he is unlikely to achieve or maintain, or have the opportunity of achieving or maintaining, a reasonable standard of health or development without the provision for him of services by a local authority under this Part;

  b) his health or development is likely to be significantly impaired, or further impaired, without the provision for him of such services;

  or

  c) he is disabled ...'

The kinds of provisions that the social services might provide are family centres that offer support to children and parents around particular problems e.g. relationship difficulties, general advice, guidance and counselling, home help, day care (s.18), and in some exceptional circumstances, cash may be given (s.17(6)).

• Children looked after

Another main duty a local authority has with regard to children is providing accommodation. Under s.20(1) of the Children Act 1989 –

> 'Every local authority shall provide accommodation for any child in need within their area who appears to them to require accommodation as a result of –
>
> a) there being no person who has parental responsibility for him;
> b) his being lost or having been abandoned; or
> c) the person who has been caring for him being prevented (whether or not permanently, and for whatever reason) from providing him with suitable accommodation or care.'

It is important to note here that this is a voluntary arrangement with the child's parents or persons with parental responsibility for the child. If a parent disagrees with the provision, then it should not be provided. Also, contrary to the media images of social workers removing children forcefully, this duty is there to help parents at difficult points in their lives. For example, consider a lone parent who has to go into hospital for a few days for an operation and has nowhere for his or her child to go. In this circumstance, s/he could contact social services who could then arrange for his or her child to be accommodated for a short period of time.

• Children in need of protection

This is perhaps the most controversial area of child care social work and comes under s.47 of the Children Act 1989; s.47(1) states –

> 'Where a local authority ...
>
> b) have reasonable cause to suspect that a child who lives, or is found, in their area is suffering, or is likely to suffer, significant harm, the authority shall make, or cause to be made, such enquiries as they consider necessary to enable them to decide whether they should take any action to safeguard or promote the child's welfare.'

This therefore means that social services have a duty to investigate any concerns regarding children who may be being abused. The types of abuse that are typically investigated fall into one of four categories: physical abuse, sexual abuse, emotional abuse and neglect. It is in these circumstances that social workers may have to go to court to seek particular orders to protect children from likely or actual significant harm. Again, it is important to mention that the courts will only make an order after consideration of the principles mentioned earlier (although the welfare checklist does not always apply). Also social workers do not like having to work against families, so where possible, they should try to consider options for the protection of the child without the need for an order.

● *What is the main Act governing Mental Health practice?*

The second area of social work practice concerns people with mental illness and who come under the Mental Health Act 1983 (MHA). The first thing you might notice about this Act is that it is quite old and as a result the government have produced a White Paper in 2000, called 'Reforming the Mental Health Act' which details its plans for new mental health legislation. This chapter cannot look at these changes other than to alert readers that they will be taking place; instead we will first consider some of the key themes and principles underpinning the Mental Health Act 1983, and then look at some of the important sections.

● *What is the definition of mental illness?*

To begin with, the MHA 1983 s.1(2) defines some terms around mental illness -

> ' ... *'mental disorder'* means mental illness, arrested or incomplete development of mind, psychopathic disorder and any other disorder or disability of mind,

> *'severe mental impairment'* means a state of arrested or incomplete development of mind which includes severe impairment of intelligence and social functioning and is

associated with abnormally aggressive or seriously irresponsible conduct on the part of the person concerned,

'mental impairment' means a state of arrested or incomplete development of mind (not amounting to severe mental impairment) which includes significant impairment of intelligence and social functioning and is associated with abnormally aggressive or seriously irresponsible conduct on the part of the person concerned,

'psychopathic disorder' means a persistent disorder or disability of mind (whether or not including significant impairment of intelligence) which results in abnormally aggressive or seriously irresponsible conduct on the part of the person concerned.'

The first point to make about these definitions is their vague and highly interpretable meanings. So for example, how does one decide what constitutes 'abnormally aggressive or seriously irresponsible conduct?' To help inform the social worker and other professionals about key areas around interpretation and practice of mental health legislation, the MHA 1983 has a Memorandum and Code of Practice that should be used in conjunction with the Act. So in terms of definitions, the MHA Memorandum explains further how to understand these terms for the purposes of assessment and intervention. The Memorandum also states that the –

' ... term *'mental illness'* is undefined, and its operational definition and usage is a matter for clinical judgment in each case' (p.7).

However, one point to note is that a person should not be seen as having a mental disorder for reasons of promiscuity, other immoral conduct, sexual deviance or dependence on drugs and/or alcohol, (MHA 1983, s.1(3)).

● *What are the principles underpinning the MHA 1983?*

The revised Code of Practice (1999) that relates to the MHA 1983 includes a number of guiding principles which are applicable for people who come under the Act. It states that people should:

- Receive recognition for their basic human rights not only under the European Convention of Human Rights but under the recently implemented Human Rights Act 1998.

- Have their individual backgrounds respected by taking into account their age, gender, ethnicity, sexuality and religion, but that this does not then lead to assumptions being made based on these characteristics.

- Receive the minimum forced intervention necessary when they require treatment or care, taking into account their own health or safety, or the safety of others.

- Be cared and treated in such a way that promotes, where possible, their self-determination and personal responsibility.

- Be discharged from any application or power for detention under the Act as soon as it is established that it is no longer justified. Hence, people should not be detained if compulsory detention is not necessary.

In addition to the above, the Code highlights other guiding principles which include:

- Communicating with patients whereby professionals ensure that everything is done to overcome any barriers that may hamper communication. For example, by using interpreters where individuals speak little or no English, avoiding jargonistic terms, and making provisions for people with a visual or hearing impairment.

- Maintaining confidentiality whereby information about a patient is not disclosed without a patient's consent unless it is in the public interest, for example where the person's health or safety may be at risk.

- The giving of information by Hospital Managers to detained patients and their nearest relatives to enable them to understand why they are in hospital and the planned care or treatment. In addition to this information, patients should be aware of what they can do if they are unhappy with the service or intervention they are or will be receiving.

● What are some of the main sections under the MHA 1983?

Admission to Hospital

Under s.131(1) of the MHA 1983 provisions are made for a patient who requires treatment for mental disorder to be admitted to any hospital or mental nursing home. What is important to note here is that admission is voluntary and that a patient may discharge him or herself at any stage. The controversy in mental health work is largely derived from patients who are 'sectioned' under the MHA 1983, which means admission is compulsory and therefore they cannot leave voluntarily. There are two main sections of the MHA which deal with compulsory admission: section 2 – admission for assessment and Section 3 – admission for treatment.

Admission for assessment

The grounds for admission for assessment under s.2 MHA 1983 are that –

a) 'he is suffering from a mental disorder of a nature or degree which warrants the detention of the patient in a hospital for assessment (or for assessment followed by medical treatment) for at least a limited period;

and

b) he ought to be so detained in the interests of his own health or safety or with a view to the protection of other persons.'

The period of detention is for up to twenty-eight days. Importantly, professionals have a great deal of discretion in what constitutes a mental disorder since mental illness, as noted earlier, is not defined in the Act but instead is left to professional judgment. This is controversial in that there are particular sections of society that are over-represented in psychiatric institutions, for example women and people from ethnic minorities. We can either conclude that these two groups are somehow more predisposed to mental illness than other groups in society, or that the current mental health system operates in such a way as to discriminate against these two particular groups.

Admission for treatment

The grounds for admission for treatment under s.3 MHA 1983 are that –

a) 'he is suffering from mental illness, severe mental impairment, psychopathic disorder or mental impairment and his mental disorder is of a nature or degree which makes it appropriate for him to receive medical treatment in a hospital;

and

b) in the case of psychopathic disorder or mental impairment, such treatment is likely to alleviate or prevent a deterioration of his condition;

and

c) it is necessary for the health and safety of the patient or for the protection of other persons that he should receive such treatment, and it *cannot be provided unless he is detained under this section*' *(our emphasi)*

As can be seen in this section of the Act, detention is more specific to the different types of mental ill-health rather than merely suffering from a 'mental disorder'.

In both these sections for admission for assessment or treatment there are usually two medical recommendations needed that agree that the grounds for admission have been met. In instances where there is an admission for assessment in cases of emergency (MHA 1983 (s.4)), only one medical recommendation is needed but the patient can only be detained for 72 hours unless the second medical recommendation is acquired within this period.

● *What is the role and what are the duties of the Approved Social Workers?*

Approved Social Workers have a very important part to play in mental health law and are the link between the service user and his or her family and the health professionals. Their responsibilities include –

- The duty to make an application (s.13(1)) for a hospital admission for a patient where in their opinion it ought to be made given the grounds for admission under the different sections of the MHA 1983 (as discussed earlier).

- The duty to interview the patient before making an application for admission to hospital (s.13(2)).

- The duty to assess the need for an application when required by the nearest relative (s.13(4)).

- The duty to take practicable steps to inform the nearest relative of a patient who is subject to an application for admission to hospital (s.11(3)).

- The power to apply for a warrant to search for and remove patients (s.135(1)) where it is believed that a person is suffering from a mental disorder and is being ill-treated, or where he is seen to be unable to care for himself.

● *Who is the nearest relative?*

Another key person in the MHA 1983 is the 'nearest relative' who can either be, in order of rank, the husband or wife, son or daughter, father or mother, brother or sister, grandparent, grandchild, uncle or aunt, niece or nephew, and in some cases non-relatives (s.26). The eldest in any category takes precedence, regardless of sex. The nearest relative to a patient has a number of rights under the MHA 1983 which include:

- The right to require a local authority to assess a patient

- The right to make an application (for admission of the patient to hospital)

- The right to be informed

- The right to be consulted

- Rights of discharge

- Right of independent medical opinion

- Right of nearest relative to nominate another relative as nearest relative

This section has only covered a small part of the powers and duties that are placed on health and social services authorities under the MHA 1983. For further reading see Rashid, Ball & McDonald (1992).

● *What Acts cover work with Young Offenders?*

The legislation that governs social work with young offenders is mainly covered in a recent Act called the Crime and Disorder Act 1998 (CDA). However, unlike the two previous sections, there is much other relevant legislation that affects young offenders and includes the Children and Young Persons Act 1933; the Children and Young Persons Act 1969; Criminal Justice Act 1991; Criminal Justice and Public Order Act 1994 and so on. Given the scope of this chapter we will only be able to consider the Crime and Disorder Act 1998.

The principal aim of the Crime and Disorder Act 1998 is to prevent offending by children and young people and places a duty on the youth justice system to have regard to this aim (CDA 1998, s.37). The youth justice system deals with offences committed by children or young people aged 10-17 years of age. Whilst this age band has not changed under the CDA 1998, it has introduced orders that can be imposed on children under the age of 10 years who commit an 'offence,' although 10 remains the age of criminal responsibility.

● *What are the objectives of the youth justice system?*

Before looking at the main sections in the CDA 1998, it is important to look at some of the principles and objectives underpinning youth justice work. Six objectives have been identified by the Home Office (1998) in their framework document for the CDA 1998.

• The swift administration of justice so that every young person accused of breaking the law has the matter resolved without delay.

This is to ensure that –

   a) the alleged perpetrator and victim do not have to endure unnecessary stress caused by slow procedures for a trial;

   b) the risk of re-offending whilst awaiting trial is minimized;

   c) early action can be taken to prevent any further offending.

- Confronting young offenders with the consequences of their offending, for themselves and their family, their victims and their community, and helping them develop a sense of personal responsibility.

    This objective aims to help young people to understand the consequences of their offending behaviour for others, in particular the victim, and to enable them to take personal responsibility for it in the hope that they are less likely to repeat it.

- Intervention which tackles the particular factors that put the young person at risk of offending and which strengthens 'protective factors.'

    Here the emphasis is on the need for a comprehensive range of local strategies that can be used to deal with offending behaviour, with the primary aim of reintegrating the young person into the community.

- Punishment proportionate to the seriousness and persistence of the offending.

    This is a complex issue where the offender, victim and the public should feel that the response by the courts, for example, fairly reflects the seriousness of the offending. To some extent this is very difficult to achieve since victims may often feel that the punishment for an offender was too lenient, whilst an offender may feel that punishment was too harsh, with the general public having a wide variation of opinion based on their views of crime and punishment. However, generally, the thrust of such recent legislation has been to reinforce punishment as a means of addressing criminal behaviour.

- Encouraging reparation to victims by young offenders.

    The emphasis here is for the young offender to take responsibility for his or her actions through reparation, like community service. The aim is to enable the young person to change their offending behaviour through this reparation and for the victim of the crime to feel that justice has taken place.

- Reinforcing the responsibilities of parents.

  Parents and guardians of young offenders are asked to take proactively some responsibility in preventing their young adolescent from offending or re-offending. Research shows that poor parenting may be associated with a young person's offending behaviour, and sometimes the parents may need support to help them manage their son or daughter.

Moving on from these six objectives we will now look briefly at five specific sections within the Crime and Disorder Act 1998 that add substance to these objectives.

● *What are some of the orders that affect children and young people?*

Local Child Curfew Schemes may be made by different local authorities as a way of preventing young children under the age of 10 years getting into trouble (s.14(1)). This can take the form of a ban on children under the age of 10 years being in a public place within a specified area during specified hours (between 9pm and 6am) unless they are with a parent or responsible person (s.14(2)).

Child Safety Orders may be made by a magistrates' court on the application by a local authority which places a child under the age of 10 years under the supervision of a responsible officer and requires the child to comply with specified requirements (s.11(1)(a) and (b)). Such an order is essentially designed to prevent the young child from behaving in a way that if he/she had been older would have constituted a criminal offence, or stop them causing harassment, alarm or distress to others.

Anti-Social Behaviour Orders are similar to child safety orders in that they are designed to prevent a child aged 10 years or above from causing harassment, alarm or distress to others not in the same household (s.1(1)(a)). The crucial difference here is that the child is of sufficient age to be tried for a criminal offence, and sentenced to a criminal penalty, should they be found to breach the conditions of the anti-social behaviour order (s.1(10)(a) and (b)).

Parenting Orders as the name suggests, are orders which courts can make that impose conditions on parents, to attend, for example, guidance or counselling sessions (s.8(4)(b)) to address their child's offending behaviour. The order can only be made where there is already a specific order in force, for example, a child safety order or an anti-social behaviour order (s.8(1)). Essentially, a parenting order is to force parents to help prevent the circumstances that led to their child's offending behaviour.

Removal of truants to designated premises is not an order but a power that the police now have under the CDA 1998 s.16(3) which states that –

'If a constable has reasonable cause to believe that a child or young person found by him in a public place in a specified area during a specified period –

a) is of compulsory school age; and

b) is absent from a school without lawful authority the constable may remove the child or young person to designated premises, or to the school from which he is absent.'

● What Acts cover the care of Adults?

This section will consider some of the legislation that is relevant for the social care of adults, in particular older people. The first thing to say here is, unlike the previous three areas where, on the whole, there is one main Act governing the area for practice, in the social care of adults there are numerous relevant sections of different Acts with some dating back to 1948. However, this section will mainly confine itself to the National Health Service and Community Care Act 1990 (NHSCCA).

Before considering the above Act, it is important to understand briefly the context of community care legislation. Prior to this Act, many adults, particularly those with learning disabilities who needed support and services, were having to be admitted to residential homes or hospitals in order for them to receive the care they needed. Some of these residential institutions were seen to have a detrimental effect on the service users through the process of 'institutionalisation.' The NHSCCA 1990 was introduced to enable care in the community of many vulnerable adults and older people who may otherwise have been admitted into a residential setting.

There are two important sections within the NHSCCA 1990 that cover the general provisions concerning community care services. s.46(1) states that –

'Each local authority –

a) shall ... prepare and publish a plan for the provision of community care services in their area.

s.46(3) goes on to define community care services:

' ... means services which a local authority may provide or arrange to be provided under any of the following provisions –

a) Part III of the National Assistance Act 1948;

b) section 45 of the Health Services and Public Health Act 1968;

c) section 21 of and schedule 8 to the National Health Service Act 1977; and

d) section 117 of the Mental Health Act 1983 ...'

The kinds of services that these different sections refer to include social work support, residential care, laundry services, meals on wheels, mental health aftercare, day care and home care which are referred to again in Chapter Five.

s.47(1) of the NHSCCA 1990 is also important in that it places a duty on the local authority to carry out an assessment of a person's need. This section states:

' ... where it appears to a local authority that any person for whom they may provide or arrange for the provision of community care services may be in need of any such services, the authority –

a) shall carry out an assessment of his needs for those services; and

b) having regard to the results of that assessment, shall then decide whether his needs call for the provision by them of any such services.'

In theory this should mean that the assessments that social workers carry out with adults in need should be 'needs-led' and therefore determined by what the service user's requirements are, rather than resource-led, where services are provided based upon what the authority has available. In practice, social services are often criticized for assessments that are based upon the latter.

As suggested above, a major issue with community care social work practice is one of the resources and the extent to which what is in the service users' interests can be secondary to what provisions are available (see Chapter Five for further discussion of this point). Unlike the Children Act 1989 mentioned earlier, there is no welfare principle where adults' needs are seen as paramount: why? Could it be that vulnerable adults are not seen by society as a priority when compared to vulnerable children, or that we all have a responsibility for children while adults should take responsibility for themselves? Consider the public outcry when a child dies because of some abusive incident or neglect, and then compare that to what happens when you hear about an older person dying in their home through hypothermia. The law usually reflects how society views situations.

As mentioned earlier there are numerous pieces of legislation that affect vulnerable adults and this is partly because the NHSCCA 1990 does not incorporate previous legislation into the one Act. Therefore, social workers need to be aware of the other relevant Acts which are briefly mentioned below.

National Assistance Act 1948 places a duty on the local authority to make arrangements for the welfare of persons (18 years and above) who are disabled, and also gives the local authority the power to remove people compulsorily from their home who are 'aged, infirm, and suffering from grave chronic disease.'

National Health Service Act 1977 places a duty on local authorities under schedule 8 to provide home help and laundry facilities to persons in need. This schedule also allows local authorities to provide services for people with physical or mental ill-health including day centres, meals, social work support, residential accommodation and aftercare.

Chronically Sick and Disabled Persons Act 1970 enables services to be provided to assist people to remain in their own homes and includes services such as equipment and home adaptations, practical help in the home, holidays, travelling, radio and TV. These services are available to people whom the local authority define as disabled and who live in their area.

Carers (Recognition and Services) Act 1995 is linked to s.47(1)(a) of the NHSCCA (cited above) and places a duty on the local authority to carry out an assessment of a carer's ability to provide care for the relevant person (s.1(1)(a) and (b)). The inclusion of carers' needs means that ' *... the interests of family, friends and neighbours who provide some essential support is not overlooked.*' (McDonald, 2001: 148).

Carers and Disabled Children Act 2000 extends carers' rights to an assessment.

This chapter has highlighted some of the important primary legislation that governs practice in the four areas of social care.

● What else do I need to know about Acts?

Here are some general points which can be made about Acts affecting social care:

● The interpretation in official guidance from government departments of how an Act is to be implemented is very important. Many practitioners use this guidance as their source of the law rather than the Acts themselves. This is fine, as long as the distinction is understood.

● What may seem straightforward in an Act can be much more complicated in practice. Especially in social and health care matters the Acts may only be able to provide the principles, not the detailed applications when it comes to balancing issues of care and control, of risk, of rights and responsibilities, and so on in any particular situation.

● Because of the way social and health care legislation has developed over the years, especially in recent times, it is important for practitioners to know whether they are acting as an individual or as an agent for some other legal authority. While you have a duty to act reasonably and with care in all your professional work, who is ultimately responsible for your actions and decisions may vary – sometimes it may be you yourself, sometimes your employer, sometimes an agency which has contracted you to work for it.

● There can be complex answers, in law, to the question 'who is my client?' While it may appear obvious who you are working with, and whom you would normally refer to as a client, it may not be strictly so in law. To be confused about whose interests are to be primarily served can lead to trouble, be it in child care, mental health, youth justice or adult community care. For example, child care social workers have run into trouble by confusing the parent rather than the child as their primary client; carers as well as dependant older people have rights which both need to have addressed; youth justice workers have to distinguish young offenders and the courts and society as their 'clients.'

- The modern tendency is for governments to set out broad frameworks for their policies in the Acts they pass, setting statutory aims or purposes for services and requiring plans to be drawn up for their delivery, with reports on how effectively the duties to provide services have been discharged. How these duties and obligations are to be fulfilled is then sometimes less prescribed than in the past, but there is a tendency for modern governments to be ambivalent about how much they want to centralise control and how much they want to delegate to others.

- The flow of legislation in the areas of health and social care has been quite rapid in recent times. There are many other Acts besides the ones mentioned in this book which affect your work, and there are others in the pipeline. For example, there is the health and safety legislation, the charity laws, the race relations laws (including the Race Relations (Amendment) Act 2001 which places a new enforceable positive duty on public authorities), and the creation of a new service – the Children and Family Court Advisory and Support Service – from 1st April 2001 under the Criminal Justice and Court Services Act 2000. More changes are also due in respect of health care and mental health, while issues around youth justice seem regularly to attract further legislation.

- The Care Standards Act 2000 relates to social care law in that its purpose is to ensure that systems exist to monitor the standards of care in children's homes and care homes for vulnerable adults and 'hospitals' that are not NHS hospitals. The Act also relates to the standards of domiciliary care arrangements for persons living in their own homes and also the arrangements made for the adoption and fostering of children. A National Care Standards Commission has been created that has the responsibility of keeping the Secretary of State informed about the provision of services, in particular about the availability of the provision and the quality of the services provided and this information is to be available to the public.

The Act brings up to date matters relating to the regulation of establishments and agencies and reinforces national minimum standards.

As you have already found out through reading this chapter, there are a number of underlying principles that relate to the application of the law to social care practice. One overarching theme is the significance of the monitoring and regulation of public services and the importance of quality standards. A good understanding of social care law is essential for good practice and therefore is relevant to quality outcomes for service users.

Chapter Four

What is Delegated Legislation?

We have seen in Chapter Three what we mean by an Act of Parliament, and that there are several key Acts which set the legal framework in which social workers and social carers carry out much of their day-to-day work. While the Acts are very important in setting the principles and boundaries of what must be done or may be done and what cannot be done, it is more detailed rules and regulations which often affect that day-to-day work. Often it is these rules and regulations which set out *how* the work is to be done. Where do all these detailed requirements come from? The answer is usually: from 'delegated legislation'. What is delegated legislation?

Well, as we saw in Chapter Two, and again in Chapter Three, and as we shall see again in Chapter Five, Acts often give certain people duties and powers. Amongst those powers sometimes can be the power to make other laws. 'Delegated legislation' is the description given to the rules, orders, regulations and byelaws made by persons or bodies under specific powers delegated to them by Parliament. Delegated legislation has the same legal force as the Act under which it is created. It has been estimated that there are twenty times as many sets of rules and regulations enacted each year as there are Acts of Parliament, which shows how significant delegated legislation can be to practitioners.

There are various types of delegated legislation.

> *Orders in Council.* These are Orders made by the Privy Council, which is a non-party political body of eminent parliamentarians, but in practice an Order in Council is generally made by the government and merely sanctioned by the Privy Council. Many Acts are brought into operation by Orders in Council (see Chapter Two).

Statutory Instruments. These are the means by which government ministers introduce regulations made by them under delegated powers. They are cited by a calendar year and number and often by a short title. For example, SI 1991 No. 1506 Children's Homes Regulations 1989 is the Statutory Instrument which sets out in detail the rules for staffing, accommodation, control and discipline, storage of medicinal products, religious observance, fire precautions and so on in children's homes. They were made by the Secretary of State for Health in exercise of specific powers conferred by various sections of the Children Act 1989.

Byelaws. This is the means through which local authorities and other public bodies, which are empowered to do so, can make legally binding rules.

Court Rule Committees. These Committees are empowered to make the rules which govern procedure in the particular courts over which they have delegated authority.

Professional regulations. Some professional bodies have delegated authority to regulate the conduct of their members by making rules which have the force of law. For example, the Law Society has power under the Solicitors' Act 1974 to control the conduct of practising solicitors.

● Who has delegated powers?

As we have seen above, there are three main groups of people who have powers to make delegated legislation: Secretaries of State of the different government departments, local authorities and a range of other bodies. When a Secretary of State wishes to exercise her or his law-making powers, the delegated legislation must be 'laid before Parliament'. This means that the proposed delegated legislation must be placed or 'laid' on the table in the House of Commons and the House of Lords for a specified number of days. There are then two ways in which it can come into force: by either a positive or negative resolution of the House. A positive resolution is when a vote is taken – although there is no debate; a negative resolution is where it comes into force after the specified number of days unless a sufficient number of MPs put their names down in order to require a vote to be taken.

Although there may be much less discussion of fundamental principles when considering delegated legislation than when discussing primary legislation – Acts – a lot of work has to go on in respect of the detail of secondary legislation. The Secretary of State will, through the officials of the relevant department, normally consult with a lot of people to try and make sure the regulations are appropriate and workable. You may find yourself contributing to the preparation of such regulations through your professional associations, trade unions, consultation documents and such like. Often drafts are circulated for comment before being finalised. It is sometimes argued that it is because professional expertise – which Members of Parliament may not necessarily have – is needed in preparing such detailed regulations, that the system for producing delegated legislation is so necessary.

Local authorities are often carrying out government policies and applying them to their local communities, but where they do have power to make byelaws they are discussed in the Council and voted on in the usual way.

Similarly, other bodies which have powers to pass delegated legislation will have systems of committees which draft, scrutinise and approve proposed regulations before they are formally passed by the body with the legal authority to do so.

● *What is the difference between direction and guidance?*

We saw in Chapter Two how politicians and policymakers turn their ideas into rules through the law-making process. But central government has other ways at its disposal for getting local government, organisations and individuals to do what it wants them to do. You may have heard the saying: 'He who pays the piper calls the tune,' and because central government controls so much of the public money in the public purse, it can control how local government, organisations and individuals spend the funds allocated to them.

Some discretion may be allowed and governments will usually want the services which they fund to be delivered in local areas in ways which are appropriate and sensitive to the characteristics of different localities. But at the same time, they may be looking for consistency, equity and common standards in the services provided for all citizens. It is often the tension between local needs and national requirements which causes difficulties between national and local government.

Voluntary organisations, although they often need public money to survive, try to protect their independence as far as possible so that they can do innovative things and meet particular needs on which the statutory services are not empowered to spend public money. Similarly, private enterprise companies can set up services in markets which they see as potentially profit-making, and many have chosen to do so in the social care sector. And so there is further potential tension between the need to encourage private enterprise while safeguarding possibly vulnerable citizens from the risk of neglect and exploitation.

All of this reminds us of what was said at the beginning of Chapter Two, that we have laws because we live in a world of relatively scarce resources and because people's interests do not always fully coincide. A current trend, therefore, has been for government not only to set the legal framework for public services but also that for the independent sector services – voluntary and private enterprise – and to use 'regulatory' bodies to license and control how services are provided.

Government brings its pressures to bear in various ways. The rest of this chapter is about these various mechanisms.

We have seen that the legal framework for social work and social care is set out in Acts of Parliament – sometimes called 'primary legislation' – and in delegated legislation – sometimes called 'secondary legislation.' Within that legislation, both primary and secondary, requirements are made upon practitioners to ensure that the law is fulfilled. So we have started to answer the question: 'what is the difference between direction and guidance?' Now let us do so more specifically.

Directions. Directions can be made under an Act of Parliament, and so is another form of delegated legislation. For example, section 7A of the Local Authority Social Services Act 1970 requires local authorities to exercise their social services functions "in accordance with such directions as may be given to them" by the Secretary of State. So when the National Health Service and

Community Care Act 1990 required, by section 46, that each local authority prepare and publish a community care plan, the Department of Health stated that it would advise the Secretary of State if it appears necessary to issue general directions to ensure that local authorities' plans are in line with national policies and priorities, that implementation is proceeding at a reasonable pace, and the Secretary of State would use powers to intervene where necessary. The message to local authorities was clear: get on with it and do it our way and in our time-scales, or else!

Approvals. Like Directions, Approvals are another form of delegated legislation, made under an Act of Parliament. While Directions place duties on authorities, Approvals give them Powers. (See Chapter Five for more details on Duties and Powers.) For example, the Health Services and Public Health Act 1968 section 45 empowered local authorities, with the approval of the Secretary of State, to make arrangements for the promotion of the welfare of old people. This rather open-ended provision is expressed in some specific possible arrangements listed in a Circular, and it is in this way that meals-on-wheels, transport for the elderly, the boarding out of elderly persons, visiting and advisory services, social work support, aids and adaptation and the provision of wardens all become legal.

Policy Guidance. Under section 7 of the Local Authority Social Services Act 1970 local authorities are to exercise their social services functions under the guidance of the Secretary of State. (section 7A giving power to issue Directions, referred to above, was added later.) When such guidance is given, it would be foolish for any authority to ignore it as it can be 'statutory guidance' which must be followed. Not many would wish to do so, as it is usually very helpful. It is written in non-legal language and helps authorities to understand what the government expects them to do under new legislation. Volumes of such guidance were issued when the Children Act 1989 and the National Health Service and Community Care Act 1990 were implemented. The guidance provided material for conferences, courses and meetings to enable authorities and professionals to make the necessary arrangements for putting the new laws into practice.

Practice Guidance. Alongside Policy Guidance from the government can go Practice Guidance from the Social Services Inspectorate (SSI). The Social Services Inspectorate is a professional division of the Department of Health. One of its purposes is "to provide professional ... advice and expertise to Ministers, the Department and the field on ... the implementation and review of social services and health policies, and the effective and efficient delivery of social services". Another purpose is "to facilitate communications between the department and the field". Numerous reports are issued each year clarifying issues, spreading good practice and reporting on inspections of services. A good example is LAC(96)7, which was a Circular which came with two documents in a pack. One document was Policy Guidance setting out the Government's view of what local authorities should be doing to implement the Carers (Recognition and Services) Act 1995, and the other document was a Practice Guide from the SSI, covering such things as the key issues in assessments of carers, what a carer's assessment might cover, and things to remember when doing an assessment of a young carer.

Circulars. A Circular was mentioned above. Circulars are being issued by Government Departments all the time. As above, their titles are abbreviated: for example, LAC – meaning local authority circular, or HSG – for Health Service guidelines. In fact, the circular mentioned above on the Carers (Recognition and Services) Act 1995 was also issued to the Health Service and so carried another reference number HSG(96)8, meaning it was the eighth HSG issued in 1996, whereas it was the seventh LAC that year. Those working in youth justice may find that they receive HOC's – Home Office Circulars – relating to offenders. Circulars are very important but their legal status varies. It is unwise to ignore them, however, especially those that contain instructions. To have disregarded the guidance contained in circulars may rebound if something goes wrong. "Even if of no legal force, it is possible that the courts might hold that a Circular gives rise to a reasonable or legitimate expectation," writes Mandelstam in 'Community Care Practice and the Law' (Mandelstam, 1995: 71).

Perhaps the answer to the question 'What is the difference between direction and guidance?' is this: they may be different in strictly legal terms, but in practice there are just different degrees of pressure which can be used to ensure that the government's policies are carried out.

● *What are Codes of Practice?*

Codes of Practice are another way of turning laws and policies into actual practice. Their precise legal status may vary and be subject to debate in the same way as some policy guidance, practice guidance and circulars. However, the legal status of such Codes is usually set out in them and they carry considerable weight. It may be helpful to think of them like the familiar Highway Code, which, issued with the authority of Parliament, under the Road Traffic Act 1988, states: "A failure ... of a person to observe any provision of the Highway Code shall not of itself render that person liable to criminal proceedings ... but any such failure may ... be relied upon by any party to the proceedings as tending to establish or negative any liability which is in question in those proceedings." Let us look at a couple of Codes of Practice which may affect social carers and social workers at times. One concerns mental health, the other young offenders.

Mental Health Act 1983. There is a Code of Practice prepared in accordance with section 118 of the Mental Health Act 1983. It was issued by the Secretary of State for Health and the Secretary of State for Wales, after consulting relevant bodies and laid before Parliament. It imposes no additional duties but provides statutory authorities, managers and professional staff with guidance on how they should proceed when undertaking duties under the Act. For practitioners, knowledge of the Code of Practice is just as important as knowledge of the Act itself. For example, section 117 of the Act requires health authorities and local authorities, in conjunction with voluntary agencies, to provide aftercare for certain categories of detained patients. The Code sets out who should organise the discussion to establish a care plan, who should be involved in the discussion, what issues should be considered in the discussion, how the plan should be recorded and reviewed. Those working in the field of mental health would have to become familiar with the Code of Practice in order to know how to carry out their legal responsibilities under the Act.

Police and Criminal Evidence Act 1984. There are four Codes of Practice which have been issued by the Home Secretary under the Police and Criminal Evidence Act 1984 and approved by Parliament. For short, they are known as the PACE Codes. They are mainly Codes of Practice for police officers, setting out how they should exercise their statutory powers to stop and search people, search premises, seize property found on persons or premises, detain, treat and question people and identify persons. Why should social workers and social carers be interested in such codes? Well, Code C – the Code of Practice for the Detention, Treatment and Questioning of Persons by Police Officers (Home Office 1995) – includes special provisions in respect of juveniles and people with mental disorders and learning difficulties. Such persons should not normally be interviewed or asked to provide or sign a written statement in the absence of an 'appropriate adult'. An appropriate adult can be a representative of the care authority if a child or young person is in care or a social worker. Those working in the field of youth justice or in Emergency Duty Teams are often called upon to act as an "appropriate adult" at police stations. It is necessary, therefore, for such practitioners to have a working knowledge of the PACE Codes of Practice as they may find themselves at any time having to ensure due process is being followed if their clients are being questioned or detained by the police.

● *What are National Standards?*

Modern governments are very keen on setting standards for the delivery of public services and for ensuring that citizens can expect certain levels of service from other providers over a whole range of provision. We are all familiar with hearing debates about food standards, the standards at football stadiums, safety standards, the standards of public transport services and so on. Social care is no exception. Just as the government sets standards for education in schools and has established Ofsted to inspect and monitor provision, so it issues its expectations of social care services and has inspectorates to monitor and report on them.

As we have seen above, the government can make its expectations clear by issuing policy guidance, practice guidance and circulars. Sometimes it makes its expectations explicit by publishing 'national standards'. During early 2001 the Department of Health consulted on the first ever national standards on adoption with a view to finalising the standards later in the year. An example is given below, relating to those working in the field of youth justice.

National Standards for the supervision of offenders in the community were issued jointly in 1995 by the Home Office, Department of Health and Welsh Office, as required standards of practice for Probation Services and Social Services Departments. In 2000 the Home Secretary issued new national standards for the supervision of offenders aged 18 years or over and the Youth Justice Board now has responsibility for issuing Standards in respect of those supervised by Youth Offending Teams. The National Standards set out in great detail what is required in bail information reports, pre-sentence reports, specific sentence reports, sentence and supervision planning, required levels of contact, achieving compliance with and ensuring enforcement of community sentences and the requirements in respect of offenders released on licence. No practitioner could operate in the field of youth justice without a thorough knowledge of these standards.

Managers of services will have their performance targets set in terms of such explicit standards, and must work to ensure that they are met.

Whether the required standards are explicit, as in the example above, or in terms of guidance and reports on best practice, the various government inspectorates will monitor and evaluate services in respect of the standards expected. The Social Services Inspectorate issue reports on a whole variety of aspects of service delivery. Sometimes these are on a specific subject, such as adoption services, with evidence taken from several agencies, in order to advise the Secretary of State on policy developments, or to address an area of concern, or to encourage the spread of best practice. Sometimes they relate to the quality of services in a particular agency. Reports of the latter kind will often point out what an agency has got to do to get its services up to standard. In cases of serious failure to meet the required standards, the agency may be placed under 'special measures' designed to bring it up to standard. In extreme cases the Secretary of State will consider exercising what are known as 'default powers' whereby those responsible for running the service can be removed and replaced by others charged to bring the service up to scratch.

Having considered the question "What is Delegated Legislation?" and looked at how important are such rules and regulations, and how central government has a variety of mechanisms for ensuring that agencies and practitioners fulfil their legal obligations to satisfactory standards, we can now turn in Chapter Five, to take a closer look at what are duties and powers.

What are Duties and Powers?

● What is the difference between duties and powers?

It is important to understand the difference between the *legal duties* and the *legal powers* of statutory bodies such as Social Services Departments. As a practitioner you need to know the boundaries of your work, i.e. how you carry out your role within the law. Similarly, those whom you aim to help need to know where they stand because powers and duties relate to their 'rights.' When we hear the word 'duty', we understand it to mean 'shall' or 'will' do something, whereas the term 'power' is less strong, indicating a 'may' or a 'could.' In other words, a *power* is far more discretionary than a *duty*. A duty to do something implies that inaction will be grounds for a legal challenge to ensure compliance.

It would be easier if this area of the law were straightforward but unfortunately it is not. Welfare legislation has suffered on occasions from poor drafting and sometimes there is a lack of clarity about the intentions of the legislators. Sometimes one could draw the conclusion that the legal drafters should have been more explicit about distinguishing between duties and powers. This issue has become more complicated over recent years because of a range of factors including raised awareness of the services that can be provided by statutory bodies and increased expectations about service quality. Yet changes in demands for services have run parallel with statutory bodies, such as social services departments, experiencing a lack of resources: there has just not been enough money to go around. Disputes as to whether a local authority or health authority 'should' provide services (a duty) have become commonplace in the last ten years; for example, in the case of R v Gloucestershire County Council and Another ex parte Barry (1997) 2 WLR 459, (1997) 2 All ER1 1997 which will be discussed in more detail later on in this chapter.

● What are the legal duties of statutory bodies?

Acts of Parliament or Statutes set out legal duties. In the context of health and social welfare they say what authorities *must* do. One example of this is the local authorities' *duty to plan*: for example, under s.46 National Health Service and Community Care Act 1990 local authorities have a duty to prepare and publish a plan for community care services and update that plan as the Secretary of State directs. All local authorities had to comply with this and you can go along to any Social Services office and ask for a copy of their published Community Care Plan. Another example is the *duty to inform*: for example, under the Chronically Sick and Disabled Persons Act 1970 s.1(2) local authorities are under a duty to inform disabled people of the services provided under s.29 National Assistance Act 1948. The local authority has a clear *duty to protect* children under the Children Act 1989 s.47(1) and a clear *duty to provide* statutory aftercare for people suffering from mental ill-health (detained under s.3 Mental Health Act 1983) following discharge from hospital (s.117 Mental Health Act 1983). Sometimes duties relate to the specific role of an agency: for example, the role of the Children and Family Court Advisory and Support Service is defined through Statute and relates to the duty to safeguard and promote the welfare of children in family proceedings and to provide advice to the courts and to make provision for the children to be represented in such proceedings.

However, it is important to distinguish between duties that relate to specific individuals and duties that are general and that relate to the population as a whole. The difference between these types of duties is that in pure legal terms breach of private duties (related to individual rights) can result in legal damages and in general it has been thought that such claims are out of place in the context of statutory welfare legislation. However, recent case law related to the interpretation of s.2 Chronically Sick and Disabled Persons Act 1970 in cases of disabled people (Barry 1997, Tandy 1998) shows that individual rights to services can be established which could be enforced if there were a failure of performance.

A specific *individual duty* can be identified by the use of words such as 'shall' and the words 'any person' – this indicates a duty towards individuals. An example of this is the duty to assess for community care services under s.47 National Health Service Community Care Act 1990 which is particularly strong if the individual being assessed is disabled under the terms of s.29 National Assistance Act 1948 and the services requested come under Chronically Sick and Disabled Persons Act 1970 s.2. However, it would be wrong to assume that an individual duty applies because an Act relates to the provision of community care services. For example, s.45 Health Services and Public Health Act 1968 relates to services for older people, but the duty is clearly general rather than specific.

General duties or target duties mean duties to the population as a whole. Often these duties relate to general arrangements such as the provision of home help services under Schedule 8 National Health Service Act 1977. The Children Act 1989 s.17 describes a general duty of local authorities to safeguard and promote the welfare of children in need and this has been interpreted as a general duty rather than a specific duty towards an individual child.

However, it may not come as a surprise to learn that the distinction between individual and general duties is not that clear. Such a distinction should not be used by local authorities as a way of not accepting their responsibilities by, for example, taking a too narrow view of what they could provide (R v Tower Hamlets London Borough Council, ex parte Bradford 1997); in this case a family with multiple problems requested rehousing and a community care and a child care assessment. Therefore a whole range of duties and powers were involved that came from different statutes. The case turned on whether the local authority should have considered housing as part of the assessment under the Children Act 1989 s.17 which placed a general duty on the local authority to safeguard and protect the welfare of children in need. The judge decided that the local authority had not approached the assessment as broadly as they should have within the terms of a general duty to safeguard children in need.

The main area where there have been disputes about individual and general duties has been assessment for community care services. There is an individual duty to assess people under s.47 National Health Service and Community Care Act 1990, but the duties to provide services pursuant to that are less specific in the legislation that has to be considered in any decisions about service provision (e.g. Health Services and Public Health Act 1968, National Health Service Act 1977). In the case of R v Islington Borough Council ex parte Rixon 1997, the judge was clear that the duty to provide services under s.29 National Assistance Act 1948 were general duties and not specific ones. Directions produced under the 1948 Act were not enough to imply an individual duty. The legal debate in cases such as these has become very complex. It is important, however, that you understand that there is more to duties than meets the eye, and it may be necessary in your practice to question whether a duty placed on the local authority through Acts of Parliament relates to the population as a whole or to specific individuals. If in doubt, it is likely to be the former but you may need to ask for legal advice if the case gets complicated.

As we have mentioned before, any interpretation of a duty has to be looked at in context. Often the word duty relates to other words such as 'the duty to assess for needs.' We know that 'need' is an extremely slippery concept and difficult to define; in fact the law does not define 'need' for us. For example, in order for the duty to provide community care services to be triggered under s.2 Chronically Sick and Disabled Persons Act 1970 there are qualifying words that are important because provision is dependent on the authority being satisfied that the need triggers a duty in them to provide their services. Need and necessity have to be established. In community care law this relates to the use of eligibility criteria that can be legally established by local authorities at Social Services Committee level to determine eligibility. Passing through the eligibility criteria is the first rung on the ladder to getting community care services; in other words duties can be qualified. Other terms that are used to relate to interpretations of key concepts are a duty to provide 'to meet reasonable requirements' (National Health Service Act 1977 s.3) and duty to investigate if there is 'reasonable cause to suspect that a child who lives or is found in their area is suffering or likely to suffer significant harm' (Children Act 1989 s.47(1)'. What 'reasonable' and 'significant' mean has to be a matter for interpretation in each case. It is no surprise therefore that challenges in judicial review often relate to the interpretation of reasonableness or unreasonableness!

Breaches of statutory duty occur when public bodies have not performed their duties as set out in Acts of Parliament. It will be a matter for interpretation by the courts whether this is the case. As we have discussed above, it is unlikely that a breach of statutory duty in welfare law will be resolved by the award of damages because of the difficulty of proving individual rights and therefore a private claim in law. If a local authority were in breach of its duty, a more likely outcome would be that the court would make an order ensuring that the local authority did comply.

● *What are the legal powers of statutory bodies?*

When we think of a power to do something, we are aware of an element of discretion: decisions could go one way or the other. Let us consider some examples of powers from different areas of social care law:

- The Direct Payments Act 1996 gives the local authority the power to offer direct payments to users who qualify for community care services. Local authorities can decide to change radically the way they manage care through use of the Direct Payments system. However, the evidence shows, for example, that the involvement of local authorities in direct payments has been slow (Bright and Drake 1999) and there is a danger that the powers will be used with certain client groups rather than with others Blanket assumptions must not be made that whole groups of people would be unable to manage direct payments (DOH 2000). It is the internal policy within social services departments backed up by practice and policy guidance that drives decisions as to whether to extend Direct Payments to more clients or not.

- A Youth Justice Worker has the power to 'breach' a person placed under Supervision if they do not comply with the requirements of a Supervision Order. The officer makes a judgment based on evidence that the offender has not complied to a degree that breach procedure must be followed; the decision is a professional one and the officer is exercising a legal power under the Powers of the Criminal Courts (Sentencing) Act 2000.

- The Mental Health (Patients in the Community) Act 1995 defines requirements that 'may' be imposed when a person is subject to supervised discharge after a period in hospital. These requirements can include that the patient should attend at particular places at set times for medical treatment or education and training. The reasons for imposing any requirements should be explained to the patient and the details should be included in the care plan. These are powers validated by the statute that can be used to support the idea of discharge from hospital under supervision.

It follows that, if local authorities have powers, it is their employees acting as agents who make decisions about other people's lives. It follows then that health and social care professionals need to know the law but they also need to have a wider knowledge of ethical theory and modes of moral reasoning so that they can apply the rules 'fairly'. At the very least they need to be able to justify why a decision has been made and show the evidence to support a decision. This is the realm of ethics – the rules controlling the conduct of people in relation to others – and not directly the remit of this book. However, at the end of the book there is some further guidance that enables the reader to follow up the discussion in more detail and the final chapter links professional practice issues to learning the law for social work and social care.

● Can legal duties be affected by lack of resources?

Case law over the past few years suggests that the legal duties placed on local authorities by statute can be affected by a lack of resources. The famous case of Mr Barry that went to the House of Lords in 1997 caused disability organisations to argue that duties had been collapsed into powers as a result of this case. In R v Gloucestershire County Council and Another ex parte Barry (1997), the courts were faced with a dilemma of a council which claimed to have insufficient resources to meet the statutory obligations that created public law rights enforceable by the individual under s.2 Chronically Sick and Disabled Persons Act 1970. In this case, following a process of Judicial Review through to the Court of Appeal and then the House of Lords, the court held that the local authority could take resources into account when deciding whether to provide services to disabled people in the community. The argument in the Barry case centred on a duty to reassess for services. Mr Barry had already received certain services that had been withdrawn owing to budget cuts.

It appears, however, that this ruling has not been followed in other similar cases that relate to different statutes. In R v East Sussex County Council ex parte Tandy (1998), the House of Lords ruled that it was wrong to reduce a package of care due to budget cuts. The Council was not entitled to consider expense when fulfilling its statutory duty to provide suitable education for a special needs child. Levels of service must be assessed on grounds of educational need – that is need according to the experts or professional opinion.

> "the difference in outcomes of these two cases shows that two different regimes, drafted at different times by different draftsmen in different fields, but using comparable words such as 'necessary' or 'suitable' can lead to markedly different results." (Schwehr, 1999: 16)

So the message is ... be careful about the exercise of duties and powers and if in doubt, seek advice!

Clearly it is easier for local authorities to limit their spending with regard to powers rather than duties, but nonetheless they should be wary of fettering their discretion by the adoption of rigid policies (Mandelstam, 1998). Fettering of discretion means applying their powers in a restricted way: for example by not informing the public of their powers and by not exercising them; for example, not using Direct Payments for specific groups of clients because it might mean using more staff time to organize and administer such a scheme.

● What are the duties and powers of individual practitioners?

When social workers do their job by exercising the duties of the local Social Services Department by, for example, removing a child under an Emergency Protection Order, they are not acting as individuals but as agents for the local authority. This status gives them protection from being sued as an individual for negligence, unlike medical personnel, such as GPs, who are considered to be working on their own and therefore need indemnity protection against the possibility of the court awarding damages if negligence should arise. Negligence actions are part of private law and relate to a duty of care being established, breach of that duty and harm occurring as a result. A legal remedy for breach of duty of care is damages. Whereas negligence actions are unlikely in social services because of the notion of agency, negligence claims are becoming increasingly common in the medical field and, it could be argued, are on the increase with the dispersal of social service functions to independent agencies. The relationship between the worker and the agency in those situations is less secure and employees are often advised by unions and professional bodies to ensure that they do have personal indemnity cover.

● How do duties and powers relate to professional practice?

Firstly, it is important that practitioners are aware of the duties of the local authorities in relation to their area of practice. Some duties will be more common than others; for example, almost every social worker will know of the local authorities' duty to protect children but may not be so sure of, for example, the duty to inform in relation to personal records. It is important that practitioners know well the policy and practice guidance that relates to statutory duties and this usually take the form of procedural manuals that are followed in certain circumstances (for example, the emergency protection of children).

The powers of local authorities are significant because they mean that the statutory body through its employees exercises power in certain circumstances. Very often these powers relate to professional decision-making and the discretion that goes with the exercise of power. Practitioners must ensure that, when they make decisions that exercise powers, they can evidence their decisions. This is an important ethical point and one that has been reinforced by the Human Rights Act 1998. Practitioners must expect to be challenged and to present a reasoned argument as to why they exercised power in the way that they did.

It is important that practitioners keep up-to-date with changes in the law and act creatively to ensure that duties and powers are appropriately applied. On occasions it may be possible to add value to the lives of service users by thinking how powers that may not be commonly used can be exercised. A good example of this is the extension of the use of direct payments through the development of a programme to support those who are interested in giving self-managed care a try.

A summary of key practice issues relating to duties and powers:

- Duties can be distinguished from powers.

- Case law interpretations of the duties and powers of local authorities has made the distinction fuzzy.

- Duties and powers relate to professional decision-making.

- The exercise of a power relates to the exercise of bounded discretion.

- Professional decisions must be based on evidence and rely on an awareness of the application of ethics in practice.

- Professional practice decisions based on the interpretation of domestic law will be interpreted in the light of the Human Rights Act 1998.

- This is a tricky legal area and you may have to ask for advice at times before you take action!

Chapter Six

How Do We Use Our Legal Knowledge in Practice?

● What is the significance of law in practice?

This penultimate chapter aims to look at some of the broader issues around social care and law, in particular how the law is applied to practice. By now you will be aware of the significance of the law for social work in terms of:

- how it defines a social worker's roles and responsibilities in any given setting or situation;

- how practice will be influenced by the various Acts that are relevant to social work and whether the local authority have a *duty*, for example, to provide an assessment or service, or whether it is a *power* which means that it is at their discretion;

- explaining service-users' rights and what they can expect from you and the agency or authority that you work for;

- the relevance of secondary legislation or delegated legislation which is derived from statute but is a means by which local authorities can carry out government policies in accordance with the needs of the local communities which they serve.

The application of law to practice is often an area that social workers struggle with, since at times their practice seems to contradict what a particular piece of law says. The reasons for this anomaly are varied and include some of the areas already discussed in this book and highlighted above. The purpose of this chapter is to look at some of the broader issues about the application of law to practice and will include the following areas:

- Social workers' values and how these can impact on how they *interpret* the law and hence how they apply the law. Also there is the need to practise in a way which is anti-oppressive, so that individuals and families benefit from the interventions and are not further disadvantaged.

• How limited resources in social services can affect practice with service-users, which sometimes means that the duties placed on local authorities do not appear to be carried out, or only partly carried out.

• The importance of work with individuals and families in partnership rather than imposing your agenda on to them.

• How social workers' feelings of vulnerability (for example, being blamed for a child being abused) can lead to 'defensive' practices which are there to protect the individual worker, and not necessarily in the best interests of the service user or adhere to the legal mandate.

• Finally, the skills one might need to integrate social work law and practice.

● What about Values and the Law?

One might wonder what part an individual's values play in the application of law to social care practice. To illustrate the significance of this point, consider the following case:

> *Daniel, aged ten, lives with his mother and two younger sisters. His father died when he was five, following a road traffic accident. Daniel's mother finds him very difficult to cope with, and has on several occasions asked for her son to go into local authority care because she cannot control him. Daniel frequently soils himself and stays out late at night. There have been complaints by the police to social services that Daniel's mother frequently hits him when she gets frustrated with his behaviour.* (Adapted from Ball, 1991).

This case might involve a social worker from a children's team intervening with this family. The reasons for this intervention might be due to two particular legal duties that are laid down in the Children Act 1989, and that have been covered in some detail in Chapter Three.

Specifically, s.17(1) of the Children Act 1989 states:

'It shall be the duty of every local authority ...

to safeguard and promote the welfare of children within their area who are in need ...'

Or, s.47(1)(b) of the Children Act 1989 which states:

'Where a local authority –

have reasonable cause to suspect that a child who lives, or is found, in their area is suffering, or is likely to suffer, significant harm, the authority shall make, or cause to be made, such enquiries as they consider necessary to enable them to decide what action they should take to safeguard and promote the child's welfare.'

The crucial difference about these two duties is that the first is looking at work with the child and his family in a 'preventative' way by looking at what resources or services might be valuable to help the family overcome their difficulties. The second approach is a more 'protective' one by viewing the child as possibly being abused, and doing whatever is necessary to safeguard his welfare. The family should still be seen as having problems that need to be addressed, but the first priority is the child's protection.

So what does this have to do with an individual worker's values, beliefs and ethics? Well, put simply, the legal mandate for the social worker would be to gather more information about this family before deciding the most appropriate course of action. Of course, in practice this is not what always happens, since what we *think* about this family's situation also comes into play. Consider, for example, how you might view this family if you had strong beliefs or experiences of bereavement and the effect it can have on family members. You might think that the source of the problem for Daniel is the loss of his father; further, you might also think that the difficult relationship between Daniel and his mother stems from the mother's grief at the loss of Daniel's father. What you might be recommending, therefore, is bereavement counselling for the family as a possible way forward.

Alternatively, consider your choice of action if you had strong beliefs and perhaps experiences of physical chastisement and you thought that no child should ever be hit, and that parents should be reprimanded for using such a method. Now your focus might be on the information that Daniel is hit by his mother, and that the most appropriate method of intervention is to protect him from possible physical abuse.

This case example illustrates how an individual social worker's particular value base can affect the initial decision-making on how a case should be approached. The law in this case does not dictate *practice*, since the application of law in social work is often left to the local authority, its agencies and its staff to work out the details for assessment and intervention.

Practice is not just based upon what we believe is right and wrong on a particular issue, but also about the values and beliefs we hold about different members of society. In short we can be oppressive in our views about women, Black people, disabled people, gay and lesbian people, and older people, and these stereotypes can affect how we practise social work with such groups.

A good definition of oppression is provided by Mitchell (1989:14):

> '*British society is saturated in oppression ... an empowering social work practice derived from such an understanding addresses itself to the powerlessness and loss which results from the material and ideological oppression of black people ... working class people ... women ... children and old people ... disabled people; and gay people ... This social work practice recognises oppression not simply in the behaviours, values and attitudes of individuals and groups, but in the institutions, structures and common sense assumptions.*'

To understand and apply law to social care in an anti-oppressive way, it is very important first to locate oneself in terms of the prejudices and stereotypes one holds about the different groups in society. If you're honest, you'll probably find that you hold several negative views about say, disabled people in society, but rather than hide from them, take responsibility for identifying and challenging this negative thinking and behaviour. Otherwise you may be likely to further disadvantage the individuals or families you work with, rather than support them.

● *What about limited resources?*

One of the most significant issues for social care is the volume of resources that is available to support individuals and families. By resources we are not only referring to the provision of day care, meals-on-wheels, accommodation for children, nursery provision and so on, but perhaps the most valuable of resources: a social worker's time.

Consider the example of Daniel that was illustrated earlier. We mentioned that one way of working with this family would be in a preventative way by looking at what support they might need to overcome their difficulties. Despite the duty under s.17 of the Children Act 1989, many social workers and social work teams often argue that they do not have the time to work in a preventative way with families because their time is taken up with child protection concerns which take priority. Whilst this argument does have some validity, from the law's point of view, both s.17 and s.47 of the Children Act 1989 are *duties*, which mean that local authorities should be providing the necessary services. Of course this is clearly not the case, since many families who should be entitled to a service sometimes do not receive one.

You might then ask what happens to local authorities who do not comply with the duties laid down by the law, in this case the Children Act 1989. Well, in many cases the law is only as good as the people monitoring it; for social work the Social Services Inspectorate, which is a branch of the Department of Health, review local authorities to make sure they are complying with the law and policies from government. If they're not, in extreme cases they can take control of the management of a local authority in order to sort it out.

Another way local authorities can be challenged is when individual service users who feel that they did not receive a fair service can go through the civil courts to challenge the decisions made by the local authority. One such case was the Barry case to which fuller reference was made in Chapter Five.

● What about partnership in practice?

One of the most important issues when working with children, adults or families is that the work is carried out in partnership with them. Partnership is a broad concept but generally involves "... a degree of humility to accept that the professionals do not have all the answers and that clients have a major contribution to make ... also being able and willing to use power to *empower*" (Thompson, 2000: 99). So in terms of applying the law to practice, it is not enough to know what the law says in any given situation, but to think about how to work with people that includes them in the decision-making process. To illustrate practice *without* partnership consider the following scenario:

> *Sarah has three children under the age of five years and has recently separated from her partner. Her oldest son Simon is three and very active, and can at times be difficult to manage. Sarah contacted social services to enquire about what support might be available to ease the pressure in caring for her three children. A social worker visited two weeks later saying she has spoken to Sarah's health visitor and knows there are problems. The worker then continued to ask questions that made Sarah feel that she must be a poor parent if she could not cope with her children. Sarah decided she did not, after all, want social work support and asked the worker to leave. The worker agreed, but said that she may be back if she had further concerns about the children. Sarah, scared and angry, shouted at the social worker. The worker responded by saying that she was worried about what impact her aggressive behaviour might have on her children, and suggested that the children might need to be protected.*

The scenario indicates how a fairly straightforward request for help can turn into something more serious due to the poor partnership skills shown by the social worker. Instead of working with Sarah to identify the problems, to negotiate possible solutions, to enable Sarah to make choices, and to allow her to feel empowered, the opposites occurred. It is not the case here that the social worker does not know the law, but on a fundamental practice level she has worked *against* the family rather than working *with* them. Remember "... although the influence of law and policy is very strong (in social work) ... laws and policies have to be interpreted – they do not spell out in fine detail what needs to be done (or indeed how it should be done)." (Thompson, 2000: 45).

● *What about vulnerability in social work?*

Social work is one of those professions where positive, constructive work with children, adults, or families is often ignored in the public eye and only those things that go wrong attract media attention. For example, there have been thousands of children over the years who have been successfully protected from abuse and harm through social work interventions, but the only reports that the public hears about are the child abuse fatalities where social workers failed to protect a particular child. This is not to minimise the child deaths, which in some cases could have been prevented, but to assert that this one-sided negative portrayal of social work can have negative consequences for social workers, particularly in how they apply the law to their practice.

As mentioned earlier, much of the law surrounding social work is broad and serves to give public authorities a wide range of powers to support their work, without specific requirements on how it should be carried out (Clark, 2000). This means that, where social workers are given, and are expected to use, their discretion about how best to support or protect individuals and/or families, instead their practice becomes defensive as a means of trying to counter doing something wrong. So in the case of Sarah and her children for example, not only was the social worker not working in partnership with the family, but she may also have been 'looking' for child care concerns as a means of protecting herself or 'covering her back'. This defensive practice can have a number of consequences for both the families involved and for the social workers.

- There may be a preoccupation by the worker with focusing only on the concerning aspects in a particular family rather than looking at their strengths as well. This is known as the deficit model of assessment rather than a holistic one, and can leave families feeling disempowered, vulnerable and dependent.

- Paradoxically, children or adults could be placed in more danger by workers who only look at issues that might obviously harm them; harm and abuse can occur from unlikely sources, and by only concentrating on a small part of an individual or family, can mean workers miss other less obvious concerns that can have a devastating impact on people, for example, children who get bullied at school.

- Individuals and families may also be more likely to be assessed incorrectly through defensive practice, which may mean that they receive interventions or services that are inappropriate and damaging; the case example of Sarah is a good illustration of this.

- Workers, rather than using their legal rights and duties responsibly, would be engaging in practice that aims to protect themselves, rather than the public whom they are meant to serve.

It is understandable, although inexcusable, that workers may engage in defensive practices; if they are confident about their skills, experience, knowledge and, of course, legislation and policy, there should be no reason to operate in this way.

● Where do skills in social work fit in?

This final section will look at the skills needed in social work that may help to bridge the gap between law and practice. Preston-Shoot, Roberts and Vernon (1998) have identified a number of relevant skills, and some of these are detailed below.

- The ability to recognise the legal mandate in a piece of social work intervention is a critical skill for good practice. In enables you to be clear about your duties and responsibilities, and helps the individuals and families you work with to know why you are involved with them and what you can offer.

- Social work is a profession where you are accountable in many ways to different people, for example to the law, to the agency for which you work, to the profession, to service users and so on. Managing this multi-accountability means that you need to be clear about your roles, responsibilities, values and knowledge base. The next chapter will look again at how these factors should be integrated in practice, suffice to say here, that understanding the law is only one component of many that you will need to understand and develop to become the confident and competent practitioner you would wish to be.

- The collection and analysis of information should be undertaken with reference to the legal components that are relevant to that particular piece of practice. So, for example, with children who you think might be suffering or likely to suffer significant harm, have you covered all the necessary detail that is required by the relevant legislation and policy?

These are only some of the skills you will need to enable you to apply the law to your practice; nevertheless they are a useful starting point from which to build.

This chapter has looked at some of the important areas that need to be considered to enable you to apply legal knowledge to social care practice. The seventh and final chapter will look at what you have learned so far and suggest a framework for learning and applying social care law, and will build upon some of the themes already covered in this book.

Chapter Seven

Where Do I Go from Here?

● What have I learned so far?

Let us re-cap what this book has attempted to convey so far. We began by saying in the Introduction that it is not easy to draw hard and fast lines between social care, social work and health care, and that in some ways it would be wrong to do so. This is because, although we as professionals tend to define ourselves by our roles, the clients we serve come to us as whole people. It is tempting, especially because of the legal frameworks in which we have to operate, to define people in terms of legal categories, but by putting people into such boxes we may abuse our legal powers or not use them as creatively as is possible. We emphasised, therefore, that learning social care law is not a simple memorizing exercise, but a dynamic process.

In *Chapter One*, we pointed out how important it is to have a knowledge and understanding of the law, and how it can help deal with conflictual situations as well as produce the potential for legal disputes. We introduced the idea of discretion in applying the law to practice together with the place values and ethics can play in exercising discretion. While the law is not necessarily always certain and is open to interpretation, we emphasized that it is important to be accurate and rigorous in the use of legal terminology. We added that it is important to keep up-to-date with changes in the law, as the law is not static, and it is a professional responsibility to update one's knowledge and understanding. At the close of Chapter One, therefore, we suggested that in learning the law it is necessary to think both logically (in order to have a reasoned approach) and laterally (in order to have a creative approach). And so, this chapter on learning the law concluded that it is about skills as well as about knowledge.

Chapter Two argued that we have to have laws to avoid chaos and to regulate how citizens behave in a world of limited resources and of differing needs and aspirations. It outlined why there are few universal laws, because of different societies' ideas about what is good for people, and then stated that this book relates only to the law of England and Wales, with our distinction between criminal and civil law. We noted what is meant by a 'jurisdiction' but also remembered the growing importance of European law. The Chapter went on to detail how our laws are made, with political ideas being turned into statutes, but also remembering the common law and judge-made law through cases which settle what the law is to be in particular circumstances. This Chapter also introduced us to the important distinction between duties and powers.

'What is an Act?' was the question addressed in *Chapter Three*. We saw that, while it is not possible for a court to go behind an Act to declare what Parliament has willed to be illegal or to change what Parliament has enacted, at times courts have to interpret what an Act actually means. We were also reminded that the Human Rights Act 1998 requires all UK legislation to be given a meaning that fits with the European Convention on Human Rights, if that is possible. If it is not possible, it will be up to Parliament to decide what to do.

This Chapter then illustrated how some statutes and the principles which underpin them came to govern the work of social care practitioners. In particular, we looked at the importance of the Children Act 1989 in child care practice, and the Mental Health Act 1983 for the mental health work (but noted that significant reform of this Act is planned). In terms of youth justice work we looked particularly at the Crime and Disorder Act 1998, but saw how this is just one of a complex set of Acts which affect practice in this area. Similarly, in respect of adult community care, we focused on the National Health Service and Community Care Act 1990, but saw how this is just part of an intricate web of legislation covering this field of social care. The Chapter ended by reminding us that what can look straightforward in an Act can be much more complicated in practice and that it is important for practitioners to be aware of who their client really is; to think about whether they are acting as an agent or as an individual; to be alert to the range of other legislation and to impending legislation which can impact upon their practice.

Having seen how Acts are also called 'primary legislation' *Chapter Four* went on to highlight the importance of 'secondary' or 'delegated' legislation. We saw that while Acts will often set out the principles and statutory framework for professional practice, delegated legislation will often set out in more detail how the aims of the law are to be fulfilled. We noted especially the powers often given to Secretaries of State (and others) to make regulations and rules and to give directions and approvals which have the same force in law as Acts. We also saw how central government has a variety of mechanisms for ensuring that agencies and practitioners fulfill their legal obligations to satisfactory standards, through the use of guidance, circulars, codes of practice and national standards.

In *Chapter Five* we returned to look in more detail at the distinction between duties and powers. We saw that they can be general or specific, that they can be directed at the population as a whole or towards individuals, and that they can be qualified at times. We were again reminded how the law is subject to interpretation, with such terms as 'reasonable,' 'significant' and 'need' requiring such interpretation in practice, and often resulting in the use of eligibility criteria in day-to-day work. This inevitably raised again the links with ethics, the place of bounded discretion, evidence-based practice and the availability of resources. Thus, we concluded that this can be a tricky legal area, and so cautionary words were added about negligence and personal indemnity.

So, how do we use our legal knowledge in practice? *Chapter Six* looked at this question by pointing out how our values can have an effect on how we interpret the law in practice. It also emphasized the importance of anti-oppressive practice, working in partnership, the significance of limited resources, practitioners' vulnerability and the dangers of defensive practice. It concluded, therefore, by re-emphasising that learning social care law is about skills development as well as about the acquisition of knowledge.

Having re-capped some of the main themes of the book, we can now address some other questions about where to go from here.

● How should I continue learning the law?

We have written this book to help newcomers in their learning of social care law. In Chapter One we focused on why you need to learn the law and how it is important to make legal principles work. This concluding Chapter reinforces that theme by stressing certain practicalities, such as making sure that you have a 'system' to make the best use of your studies. It is advisable to devise your own system for the compilation of notes and the storing of information. Technological developments have meant that it is not always necessary to store large amounts of paper, but whatever way you do it, make sure that it works for you. Learning the law requires a systematic approach to information retrieval. This Chapter also reminds you of the process of learning; this means how you can harness knowledge, skills and values and how you can use targeted reflection to be your own judge about your progress and what you still need to learn.

It is said that first impressions count for a lot. Consider how you feel about learning the law now – do you feel overwhelmed and perhaps confused at what appears to be a mass of detail expressed in a formal language? Or, do you feel confident that you have a grasp of some of the general principles and know that you have set up a system of notes and references that will provide you with a resource for future practice? Nobody (even the lawyer who practises every day) knows all the law 'off by heart'. However, in order to be a good practitioner in social care, it is important that you do know how and where to access the information you need.

You need to have a sound knowledge base of social care law, but knowing the law is only part of it. As a social care practitioner you will have to make decisions that relate to the wellbeing and quality of life of other people and this is a big responsibility. When you apply your knowledge, you will also be using a number of skills, such as communication skills, working with others and being able to apply your knowledge in practice. These skills are learned as we go through life but they do need to be sharpened and honed by continuing personal and professional development. As your confidence and practice wisdom increases, you will find that you will use these skills automatically. At the same time, it is important that you develop skills in managing your own learning and furthering your own knowledge and skills base. One way to do this is to use constructive reflection as a way of checking out how much you have learned and where you need to develop further. Reflection is more than day-dreaming or the occasional thought; it is a structured way of managing your own learning that needs practice. There are a number of useful texts that can help you to do this, such as Boud et al (1985) *Reflection: Turning Experience into Learning*, and Ghaye (1996) *An Introduction to Learning through Critical Reflective Practice*.

● *What areas should I concentrate on first?*

If you have read this book from the beginning, one of the many things we have highlighted are the four specialist areas in social care. These areas include work with children, adults, young offenders, and those with mental health problems. These four areas were chosen because they represent the mainstream areas of social care practice. They have also been divided in this way because it reflects how we have taught social work students over the years; structuring the teaching in this way has enabled the teaching to be focused and relevant to particular students' interests. However, we have often been asked by students why they need to learn all four areas of law if they simply want to practise in a child care team, for example. The answer to this question relates to the one above, and warrants some discussion about whether law should be taught as a specialist area or whether students need to learn more general areas.

Instead of looking at this question in terms of law, it may be useful to think about the service users with whom social carers engage. Generally, people do not present themselves to social services and other agencies with problems that fit neatly into little boxes. If they did, each social work team could work with their service users without having to refer them on to other professionals, agencies or organis-ations. The reality of social work practice is that service users often present with complex, multidimensional problems which can include elements that are covered by some or all of the four main specialisms. To illustrate this point, consider the following scenario:

Ravinder is the mother of two children, Roshan (10) and Nina (6). They all live in a small house with Ravinder's mother who has several health problems including dementia. Ravinder has come to social services because she feels at the end of her tether; her oldest child Roshan seems to have joined a local gang known to engage in petty crime. Ravinder is worried that her son will end up in crime unless someone can help her to intervene. She is also the sole carer for her mother and is finding it difficult to cope with meeting her needs as well as her children's needs. For example, she cannot trust her mother with the cooking because she recently forgot the stove was on and nearly set fire to the house. Nina is also a concern since her school has contacted Ravinder saying that Nina may need specialist support due to a developmental delay in speech.

If we deconstruct this scenario, we can see that the problems within this family may be relevant to childcare social workers, particularly in terms of Roshan's behaviour and Nina's developmental delay. Youth offending teams may also be involved due to Roshan's petty offences, and may be able to help Ravinder curb his delinquent behaviour. Adult teams may also have a role in supporting Ravinder as a carer for her mother, as well as providing direct support services for her mother aimed at alleviating her health-related problems and thereby helping her retain her independence.

As we have already discussed in this book, there are different pieces of legislation and policies that are relevant for particular people with particular problems. To go back to the question cited earlier as to why students need to learn general areas of social care law, it should now be evident that individuals and families would be disadvantaged if social workers did not have this knowledge and did not know what services, provisions and assessments people may be entitled to. This is why social workers are trained to cover different areas of social work law, so that if Ravinder presented herself to social services, the childcare social worker would know how youth offending and adult teams, as well as the children's team, could help this family.

Another important reason for learning law generally rather than simply focusing on a specific field is related to the concept of anti-oppressive practice. Social care teaching and practice generally are underpinned by the principles and values that recognise that society has different groups who experience oppression, discrimination and prejudice. These groups include black people, women, disabled people, gay and lesbian people, people suffering from mental ill health and older people. Hence, simply knowing about a particular piece of legislation, like the Children Act 1989 for childcare practice, is not enough. There also needs to be an awareness of anti-discriminatory legislation.

This book cannot go into any detail about anti-discriminatory law since each area, like gender and discrimination, is complex. Instead, as an introduction to the subject, students need to be aware that there are several key Acts that are cited when referring to anti-discriminatory law. These Acts include the Sex Discrimination Act 1975, the Race Relations Act 1976, the Disability Discrimination Act 1995, the Race Relations (Amendment) Act 2000 and the more general but no less significant Human Rights Act 1998. These Acts offer protection to different individuals and groups in society who are disadvantaged due to a multitude of reasons. The important point here is that the social worker becomes familiar with these pieces of legislation, since they underpin the specialist areas of social work practice.

Another important point that relates to the above is that not all disadvantaged groups in society are protected from discrimination by legislation. For example, gay and lesbian people do not have an Act which represents and protects their rights. Indeed the opposite may be true, with the Local Government Act 1988 (s.28) seen by some as discriminating against lesbian and gay people by preventing any promotion of homosexuality in schools and other statutory settings.

Finally, thinking of the question about what areas you should concentrate on first brings us neatly to the nature of this book. This book has covered some of the fundamental questions related to learning social care law, for example, 'what do we mean by the law'? It has then gone on to cover the more specialist areas that typify social care practice to date. Learning the general elements of law and moving into the specialist areas of social care law should enable students to develop an overall knowledge base that is a foundation for further training and practice. So, start from where you are now, whatever point that may be, and keep building up your knowledge and skills. Our experience suggests that your motivation will be strongest if you follow a 'need to know' principle. When a question arises, in practice or in your studies, then you need to know the legal information or background to that question. Search it out. It will probably be more interesting and easier to remember if you can attach it to an actual experience. But don't fall into the trap of thinking that you have covered the law for every similar situation from this one experience. We stress again that the law is dynamic and you need to locate that experience in its particular context to 'assist' not to 'govern' your thinking about any future similar situation. Armed with some of the general principles and approaches included in this short book, we hope you now have a map to help you plot your route through whatever legal issues you come across.

● *Where do I look for information?*

There are several sources from which you can obtain helpful legal information. However, you should always check the date when the information was compiled. We know that the printed word in this book can easily become out-of-date, while advising you of the importance of keeping up-to-date; hence, in Chapter Three, while highlighting the current significance of the Mental Health Act 1983, we did point out that major reform of mental health law has been proposed.

- ● *Books*. Books are still an important source of legal information. In recent years there have been several authoritative writers specialising in social care law whose books have become standard texts in this field. Included among them are:

  Braye, S. and Preston-Shoot, M. (1997) 'Practising social work law' (2nd ed.), Basingstoke : Macmillan

  Brayne, H. and Martin, G. (1999) 'Law for social workers' (6th ed.), London : Blackstone

Cull, L. and Roche, J. (eds.) (2001) 'The law and social work: contemporary issues for practice', Basingstoke: Palgrave

Vernon, S. (1998) 'Social work and the law' (3rd ed.) London: Butterworths

● **Libraries.** Libraries can be useful sources not only for books but also for those many other documents to which we have referred, such as Acts of Parliament, Statutory Instruments, White Papers, Green Papers, Regulations, Circulars, Policy Documents. If you have access to a Law Library, it can be useful to get to know the specialist librarian, who can guide you through the maze of materials and advise you on current, up-to-date literature.

● **Journals.** The journals in libraries and offices can be helpful in several ways. Because they come out more regularly than new editions of books, they can be more up-to-date with changes in the law and in reporting important cases. They can also include articles discussing potential issues or setting out the background to legal problems which have arisen in practice. Additionally, they can alert you to current debates around proposals for changing and developing the law. Among the journals you may wish to refer to are:

• British Journal of Social Work

• Community Care

• Social Policy and Administration

• Social Welfare Law

● **Websites.** Probably the quickest most up-to-date sources of information are websites. Legislation and government publications can be accessed via the web, and you may find it useful to note:

Acts of the UK Parliament – http://www.hmso.gov.uk/ac.htm
Court Service Website – http://www.courtservice.gov.uk
The Law Commission – http://www.lawcom.gov.uk.homepage.htm
UK Statutory Instruments – http://www.hmso.gov.uk/stat.htm

- **Agency documents.** As we have seen already, especially in Chapters Four and Five, agency policy documents, guidance notes or codes of practice are often themselves local expressions or interpretations of the law. As long as you don't confuse them with the actual law itself, they are often a good source of explaining how the law is to be applied in your area. They can express in simple language how the duties and powers of the agency are to be fulfilled at grassroots level. Similarly, leaflets and handouts can be ways of communicating in straightforward terms the rights of service users. These often include the services which can be provided, any contributions to costs which may be necessary, complaints and appeals procedures, processes which have to be undertaken and so on, all of which are vital to the practical application of the law.

● What is our final message?

We have written this book because of our experience of seeing students and practitioners struggle with legal aspects of their studies and practice. We have observed how some have come to their learning and practice without some necessary building blocks, and therefore we have tried to set out some of the basic foundations. We have tried to be constructive and encouraging in our approach, and to recognize that learning social care law is a continuous process requiring an approach to learning that is both systematic and reflective. Above all, we have emphasized that learning social care law is not an exercise in memorising only, but a dynamic process which we sum up in the following diagram, which sets *practice* at its centre, recognises that *values and beliefs* are involved, and sets *legislation* in dynamic interplay with the interpretation of the law in *case law, policy* and *guidance.*

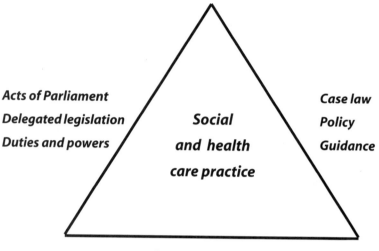

Acts of Parliament
Delegated legislation
Duties and powers

Social and health care practice

Case law
Policy
Guidance

Values, beliefs and ethics

With this 'picture' in mind, your approach to your learning will be an individual process, which brings together all these elements in an iteractive way.

We wish you well in your ongoing explorations as you pursue learning social care law.

References

Audit Commission (1994) *'Seen but not heard: co-ordinating community child health and social services for children in need'*, London: HMSO

Ball, C. (1991) *'Child care law'* (3rd ed.), Norwich: UEA

Boud, D., Keogh, R. & Walker, D. (1985) *'Reflection: turning experience into learning'*, London: Kogan Page

Bright, A. and Drake, M. (1999) *'People with learning difficulties and their access to direct payment schemes'* York: Joseph Rowntree Foundation

Clark, C.L. (2000) *'Social work ethics: politics, principles and practice'*, London: Macmillan Press

DoH (1989) *'Caring for People: Community Care in the Next Decade and Beyond, CMND 849'*, London: HMSO

DoH (1998) *'Mental Health Act: memorandum on Parts I to VI, VIII and X'*, London, HMSO

DoH (1999) *'Mental Health Act: revised code of practice'*, London: HMSO

DoH (2000) *'Community Care (Direct Payments) Act 1996: Policy and Practice Guidance'*: London, HMSO

DoH (2000) *'Reforming the Mental Health Sct'*, London: HMSO

Ghaye, T. (1996) *'An introduction to learning through critical reflective practice'*, Newcastle Upon Tyne: Pentaxion

Home Office (1995) *'Police and Criminal Evidence Act 1984'* Section 66, Code of Practice, Code C, (Third Edition) London: HMSO

Home Office, Department of Health and Welsh Office (1995) *'National Standards for the Supervision of Offenders in the Community'*, London: Home Office

Home Office, 'National Standards for the supervision of offenders in the community,' (2000), London: Home Office

Kolb, D. A. (1984) 'Experiential learning: experience as the source of learning and development', London: Prentice-Hall

Mandelstam, M. & Schwehr, B. (1995) 'Community care practice and the law', London: Jessica Kingsley

Mandelstam, M. (1998) 'An A-Z of community care law', London: Jessica Kingsley

McDonald, A. (2001) 'Care in the community' in Cull, L.A. & Roche, J. (2001) (eds.) 'The law and social work: contemporary issues for practice', Basingstoke: Palgrave

Mitchell, G. 'Empowerment and opportunity' in Dalrymple, J. & Burke, B. (1995) 'Anti-oppressive practice; social care and the law', Buckingham: Open University Press

Preston-Shoot, M. Roberts, G. and Vernon, S. (1998) 'Social Work Law : from interaction to integration', Journal of Social Welfare and Family Law, Vol 20(i) p65-80

Rashid, S.P., Ball, C. & McDonald, A. (1992) 'Mental health law' (2nd ed.) Norwich: UEA

Schwehr, B. (1999) 'Local Authority Rationing in the Provision of Services', Public Law Group, Rowe and Maw Solicitors, London

Social Services Inspectorate (1995) 'Children's Services Plans: An Analysis of Children's Services Plans 1993/94', London: Department of Health

Thompson, N. (2000) 'Understanding social work: preparing for practice', London: Macmillan

Utting, W.B. (1991) 'Children in the public care: a review of residential child care', London: HMSO

List of Statutes

Care Standards Act 2000
Carers and Disabled Children Act 2000
Carers (Recognition and Services) Act 1995
Child Care Act 1980
Children Act 1989
Children and Young Persons Act 1933
Children and Young Persons Act 1969
Chronically Sick and Disabled Persons Act 1970
Crime and Disorder Act 1998
Criminal Justice Act 1991
Criminal Justice and Court Services Act 2000
Criminal Justice and Public Order Act 1994
Direct Payments Act 1996
Disability Discrimination Act 1995
Disabled Persons (Services, Consultation and Representation) Act 1986
Health Act 1999
Health Services and Public Health Act 1968
Human Rights Act 1998
Local Authority Social Services Act 1970
Local Government Act 1988
Mental Health (Patients in the Community) Act 1995
Mental Health Act 1983
National Assistance Act 1948
National Health Service and Community Care Act 1990
National Health Service Act 1977
Police and Criminal Evidence Act 1984
Powers of Criminal Courts (Sentencing) Act 2000
Race Relations Act 1976
Race relations (Amendment) Act 2000
Road Traffic Act 1988
Sex Discrimination Act 1975
Solicitors Act 1974

List of Cases

R v Avon County Council, ex parte M (1994) 2 FCR 259 (QBD)

Birmingham City Council v H (No. 3) (1994) 2 WLR 31

R v Cambridge Health Authority, ex parte B (A Minor) (1995) 1 FLR 1055

R v East Sussex County Council, ex parte Tandy (1998) 2 AllER 769 (HL)

R v Gloucestershire County Council and Another, ex parte Barry (1997) 2 WLR 459 (1997) 2 AllER 1

R v Islington Brough Council, ex parte Rixon (1997) 1 ELR 477 (QBD)

R v Tower Hamlets London Borough Council, ex parte Bradford (1997) 29 HLR 756 (QBD)

Index

Direct Payments Act 1996, 64
Direct Payments, 64, 66, 68
Disability Discrimination Act 1995, 14, 84
Disabled Persons (Services, Consultation and Representation) Act 1986, 14
Discretion, 10, 37, 52, 60, 64-69, 75, 78, 80
Duties –
    general, 10, 21, 25, 27, 29, 31-33, 39-40, 45-48, 50, 56, 59, 60-71, 73, 76, 79, 80, 87, 88
    to plan, 26, 27, 61
    to inform, 61, 67
    to protect, 33-34, 61, 67
    to provide, 61

E

Eligibility criteria,63, 80
Emergency Protection Order, 66,
Ethics, 9, 10, 65, 67, 68, 71, 78, 80, 88
European Convention on Human Rights, 10, 11, 19, 21, 29, 36, 79
European law, 20, 21, 79
Evidence and procedure, 11

F

Family Proceedings Courts, 20

G

General duties, 61-63
General Social Care Council, 25
Green Papers, 21, 86
Guidance, 27, 47, 52-58, 80, 87, 88

H

Health Act 1999, 15
Health Services and Public Health Act 1968, 44, 54, 62, 63
House of Commons, 22, 51
House of Lords, 22, 24, 51, 65, 66
Human Rights, 18, 36
Human Rights Act 1998, 10, 11, 19, 24, 29, 36, 67, 68, 79, 84

I

Indemnity, 66, 67, 80
Individual –
    duties, 61-63
    liberty, 19
    rights, 18, 64
Interagency work, 15
International law, 18
Interpretation, 10, 12, 14-16, 24, 28, 35, 47, 50, 61, 63, 64, 68, 69, 75, 78-80, 87

J

Judicial review, 13, 63, 65
Judiciary, 24
Jurisdiction, 20, 79
Jurists, 18

L

Law Reports, 24
Law Society, 51
Legal –
    persons, 21
    precedent, 16
    principles, 13, 16, 24, 30, 79, 81
    references, 12, 24
    remedy, 67
    systems, 19, 20
Local authorities, 10, 14, 20, 21, 25-27, 32-33, 42, 44-46, 51-56, 60, 62, 64-73
Local Authority Social Services Act 1970, 25, 53, 54
Local child curfew schemes, 42
Local government, 26, 52, 53
Local Government Act 1988, 84

M

Magistrates' courts, 20, 42
Meals-on-wheels, 45-46, 54, 73
Mental disorder, 34, 35, 37-39
Mental Health Act 1983 –
    general, 12, 16, 25, 34, 35, 37-40, 44, 56, 61, 79, 85
    admission for assessment, 37, 38
    admission to hospital, 37